CW00819498

THE GALWAY
CONNEMARA

Copyright © 2024 by Elaine Heney

All rights reserved. No part of this publication may be reproduced, stored or transmitted in any form or by any means, electronic, mechanical, photocopying, recording, scanning, or otherwise without written permission from the publisher. It is illegal to copy this book, post it to a website, or distribute it by any other means without permission. This novel is entirely a work of fiction. The names, characters and incidents portrayed in it are the work of the author's imagination. Any resemblance to actual persons, living or dead, events or localities is entirely coincidental. Written by Elaine Heney and R. Ryan. Published by Grey Pony Films.

www.elaineheneybooks.com

THE GALWAY CONNEMARA

The Autobiography of an Irish Connemara Pony

Saddlestone Pony Listening School

Sinead and Strawberry
Roisin and Rhubarb
Conor and Coconut
Fiona and Foxtrot
Saddlestone Quiz book

The Connemara Adventure Series

The Forgotten Horse
The Show Horse
The Mayfield Horse
The Stolen Horse
The Adventure Horse
The Lost Horse

The Coral Cove Series

The Riding School Connemara Pony
The Storm and the Connemara Pony
The Surprise Puppy and the Connemara Pony
The Castle Charity Ride and the Connemara Pony
The Shipwreck and the Connemara Pony
The Christmas Connemara Pony

Horse Books for Kids

Listenology for Kids age 7-14
Horse Care, Riding and Training for kids 6-11
Horse Puzzles, Games & Brain Teasers for kids 7-14
P is for Pony – ABC Alphabet Book for Kids 2+

Horse Books for Adults

Equine Listenology Guide
Dressage Training for Beginners
The Listenology Guide to Bitless Bridles
Horse Anatomy Colouring Book

Welcome to the story of Lir, the Connemara pony. This book is set in Ireland and includes Irish names. Here is a pronunciation guide:

- Oisin Lir Storm – OSH-een Lear Storm
- Malley - Mal-y
- Delaney - De-LANE-y
- Erin - Air-in
- Lucy - Loo-see
- Dougal - Doo-gull
- Seamus - SHAY-mus
- Sean - Shaw-n
- Dinny - DIN-y
- Fiona - Fee-O-nuh
- Conor - CON-ar
- Laura – LAW-rah
- Donal – DOUGH-nal

- Siobhan – SHIV-awn
- Bridget - BRIDGE-it
- Aoife - EE-fa
- Deirdre - DEAR-drah
- Rory - ROAR-e
- Meave - MAY-VH
- Cillian - KILL-i-an
- Aine – AWN-ya
- Flynn - Flin
- Cormac - COR-mack
- Cara - Car-a
- Finn - Fin
- Aidan - Ay-den

History of the Connemara Pony

The Connemara Pony comes from Connemara, Co. Galway in Ireland. Connemara is a wild and rugged place, known for its dramatic landscapes, peat bogs, dry stone walls, lakes, mountains and beautiful scenery. The challenging climate and rocky landscapes have shaped the Connemara pony into a resilient breed, renowned for its hardiness.

Some people believe that the Connemara originated from Scandinavian ponies introduced to Ireland by the Vikings from the eight to eleventh centuries. In 1588, more than 17 ships of the Spanish Grand Armada were shipwrecked over the west coast of Ireland. Legend says that some of the shipwrecked Spanish horses mixed with local ones in Ireland, helping to create the Connemara breed we know and love today.

Connemara ponies are incredibly smart, sensitive, friendly and quick to learn. This makes them great for many horse sports like jumping, dressage and more. They are one of the bigger pony breeds, usually standing between 12.2 and 15.2 hands high. To be eligible to be a registered Connemara pony, a Connemara must be under 14.2 hands to fit the breed standard.

Ponies over 14.2 hands are often called 'oversized Connemaras'. Connemara crosses are also popular these days, with one parent being a Connemara pony, and the second parent being a different breed.

Connemaras are similar to all other horses and ponies, reaching maturity at a minimum of 5.5 years for a mare and 6 years for a colt or gelding, with some ponies not reaching full skeletal maturity until eight years of age. Connemara ponies can live into their 30s. Most Connemara ponies are grey or dun, but they can also be other colors.

Historically, Connemara ponies were used to help on Irish farms, carrying turf, pulling carts and ploughs. Today they enjoy international demand and can be found in countries across the globe, showing how popular and versatile the breed is.

'Capall le ceansacht' is an old Irish saying. It means that a horse should be handled with gentleness.

Chapter 1

I stared out over the wild, rugged Atlantic coastline, the wind whipping my long, steel grey mane. I could see the blackthorn trees sway in the gentle breeze in the field that sloped away from my own down to the shore. The dancing waves were cast in pink hues as the dipping sun lapped lazily against the sand. For me, Galway was the centre of the world. Or at least my world. Behind me I heard a munching sound and turned to see Quinn making his way slowly up the hill towards me, snuffling at the lush summer grass as he went.

"What are you looking at?" he asked.

"The most beautiful place I could ever see," I sighed contentedly.

"It looks like sand to me," he replied.

I snorted a little at him. "I suppose it's both, but to me, it is one of the most beautiful things I have seen. Wild and free and home."

"You were born near here, weren't you?" he asked coming to stand beside me. "In Galway I mean."

"I was," I replied rather proudly. "Yes, indeed I was."

***

My first memory is of sweet-smelling dry grass. It smells, I'm told, like fine tea, although I always think it smelled more like good hay. Meadow hay, with no dust in it. I remember lying in it, the grass feeling warm and dry under me as I dozed in the sunshine, my mother grazing at my side.

That's my first real memory, but my mother told me that I was born in much different circumstances. In fact I was born in one of the greatest storms she had ever witnessed. Lightning lit the sky as I took my first breath and the only sound louder than the clashing thunder was the roaring sound of the waves, crashing on the shoreline below our paddock.

It's no wonder then that I was named after a great warrior, the god of the sea and the dramatic weather I was born during. My name is Oisin Lir's Storm, or Lir for short and I am a pure bred Irish Connemara pony.

I spent my early days playing with the other foals, running around, bucking and playfully nipping at each other. There were five of us; myself, Erin, Malley, Shem and Delaney.

Often one of us would lift our head for no reason and run, just for the fun of it, just to feel the wind rush past our ears and pull at our fluffy tails. Then the rest of us would join in then and our mothers would sigh and trot after us, often complaining that we should slow down.

Sometimes we'd run for a good reason. I remember once spying a flapping bag caught in the hedge, twirling in a gust of wind. It sent my heart racing and I spun away from it, snorting and charging across the field as fast as I could, calling for the others to follow me away from the clear danger we were in. I remember stopping at the furthest point of the field, making myself look as big as possible as I stood and snorted at the bag, my tail held high and quivering.

"It's only a bag," my mother reassured me when she nudged me with her soft muzzle. "Just some of the human's rubbish caught in the wind."

I wasn't convinced. I watched that bag warily for hours as I nibbled at the grass, convinced it was going to try and eat one of us.

As we grew bigger we began to feel comfortable leaving our mother's sides for longer and longer periods of time. I explored the field and played with

Erin, Malley, Shem and Delaney in the summer sunshine, always knowing I could run back to my mother if I felt worried or took one of my games too far.

I often found myself up on the ridge watching the sea and sand stretch out below me. I wondered what the yellow soil would feel like under my hooves. Would it be fun to canter on? What would the waves feel like? When it was hot and the sun was shining down, I'd dream of cooling off in the lapping waves and splashing in the water.

I didn't really like the rain. Especially when it was cold and the wind was strong too. During a storm we all huddled together by the blackthorn bushes with our haunches facing the wind and rain.

Every morning, Jack, the human who took care of us, would visit us to check our water was full and that we had enough grass.

One day later that summer, an older mare called Blackthorn Bay Fiona arrived into our field. She was a twenty year old, 14.2 hands in height and a full Connemara mare, who had delivered many prize-winning foals. She had grey hairs growing around her bay muzzle and a wise look in her eyes. Soon she became known as just Nana, and Erin, Malley, Shem, Delaney and I loved her. She was kind to us all and she felt like a second mother. A story teller, a teacher. I often felt like there was nothing in the whole world Nana didn't know.

The field we lived in was large and open, a gentle sloping carpet of lush, green grass. From the top of the field, we could see the beach and the sea. At the bottom, the blackthorn bushes and wild briars would shelter us from the wind and rain. It was a perfect home. Beside it was another slightly smaller field with the same little slope. I never thought much of that field as we all ran around together, that was until we came to be weaned and separated from our mothers.

We noticed one morning that some white, furry animals had been put in the field next door. They were small with fluffy bodies and black faces. When we crept over to the fence to investigate them, they made an odd 'BAA' sound sending us scattering towards our mothers in fright.

"What are they?" I asked, hiding behind my mother.

"Sheep," she explained. "They won't hurt you. They're there to stop the grass growing too tall."

"Why?" I asked, peeking around her legs at the white sheep.

"Well, I expect they want to have less lush grass on the field before we are put in there."

"We're going in there?" I asked, still watching the sheep warily.

"Something like that," she said, nuzzling me.

Looking back, I think she knew what was coming, but she didn't say anything then. I had no idea that we were beginning the process of weaning, that we would be learning to leave our mothers. However that was what was happening.

Once every few days, Jack would bring me, my mother and some of the other mares and foals up to the yard. Jack put a headcollar on me and asked me to walk around beside him. It was confusing at the start, but after a few sessions, I started to figure it out. I could walk and stop, and turn left and right, echoing how Jack moved his feet. I could see Jack was proud of me. I was proud of myself too. I felt suddenly bigger and wiser, as if I was starting to understand the world.

One morning, we were taken back to our usual field, but instead of being turned loose together, my mother was put in the adjoining field.

At first, I panicked and called to her over the fence, but I quickly realised we could still touch noses over the fence and even groom each other. Erin, Malley, Shem and Delaney were still in with me and thankfully so was Nana. It seemed very strange, but I felt safe at the same time.

That first night, I stuck close to the fence and to Nana. She seemed to instinctively know I felt nervous and often gave me a reassuring nuzzle.

"It's not so bad," she said. "Your mother is just there."

"I know," I replied with a sigh.

"Did I ever tell you I knew your grandfather?" Nana asked, suddenly changing the subject.

I looked at her with wide eyes. "No."

"Oh, I did, he was the top Connemara show horse in Ireland; really handsome, kind, smart and brave.

Why, he won the 2004 All Ireland Championship in Dublin."

I stared at her. "Really?"

"Yes, really. Do you know how I know all of that?" she asked. I shook my head. "Because we moved to a new field beside our mothers on the same day, just like you are now," she looked at me kindly.

"Once we had grown used to being on our own we were sold together to Jack, who owns this farm, by Julie, who bred us. Julie taught Jack the gentlest way to show young foals how to be independent and no longer need their mothers to mind them. She said that kind weaning builds brave horses. Horses who don't learn fear from the start."

"Do you think Julie was right?" I asked Nana.

"What do you think?" she stood up tall. "Do you think I'm scared?"

"No," I replied.

"Then it worked," she added giving me a nudge.

Over the next few days, we settled into our new world. I still went to the fence to greet my mother and to nuzzle her, but I began to feel confident being away from her. Soon the fence visits became less and my time with my friends more and more. We had weaned ourselves and did it with no stress and no fear. Nana was right, it was a good way to create brave horses.

Chapter 2

Our field had a post and rail fence between us and our mothers, but the rest of the field boundary was a large drystone wall. We would occasionally go to the wall and look out over it, but it was our woolly sheep friends who led us on our exciting adventure beyond the wall.

The sheep were moved back into our field soon after we were weaned from our mothers. I discovered they were quite friendly, if a little skittish. At first, we tried to play with them, but they would run away from us and bleat.

One thing they did like to do though was huddle by the wall at the top of the field. Some of them even took to scrubbing themselves on the stone. This was fine until one morning, when they dislodged several of the stones causing the wall to tumble a little. We quickly jumped away snorting, but the sheep promptly hopped over the little wall and disappeared.

Seeing them go, we decided to follow and find out what was on the other side of the wall. Nana was running around shouting at us, but we didn't listen, each of us following the next over the wall with a little hop.

Beyond the wall was a trail that wound down the steep slope towards the beach. We followed it and each other, weaving our way through dunes of rough, scrubby grass that was not nearly so nice to eat as the lush green blades that grew in our field.

The little beach we found ourselves on seemed enormous at the time, although when I think back to it, it was more a quiet cove than an expansive beach.

Curved, with soft sand and calm lapping waves, it was the perfect place to play. We cantered around on the sand, rolled in it, tossing the soft grains over our backs. We even waded into the water, snorting at the little waves, and digging in the surf, causing it to splash around. I stuck my mouth in it to drink but found it salty and raised my head up, shaking it, the water dropping from my lips back to the sea.

Erin started to run, racing around on the sand and soon we were all doing it, darting about and bucking. We were free, really and truly free. We could go anywhere, do anything. I finally felt the yellow soil, or sand as I now know it is, under my hooves, sinking and soft.

I lay down and rolled in it, feeling the sand sink into my coat and massage my muscles as I rolled on my back from side to side. I felt the warm water on my body as I splashed in the sea. It was as wonderful a feeling as I thought it would be. It felt like we were there for days, the lazy afternoon hours stretching on and on, but in reality, I think we were out only for a few hours at most.

As the sun started to set Jack arrived, laughing, and shaking his head once he had assured himself that we were all there and safe.

"This is not your field," he called to us. "Come on, it's supper time."

Jack held up a large bucket and rattled it, the sound of food grabbing our attention. The beach was fun, but it wasn't a very good place to find food. My tummy rumbled and I eyed the bucket, thinking of feed and the lush grass of our field. I'm not sure who moved first, but as soon as one of us did we all went, like one of the waves we had played in that afternoon.

We trotted through the sandy dunes towards Jack and that feed bucket. Jack handed out a few handfuls of feed from the pail and then shook it again to keep our attention before walking away along the track, us following him like a train.

The wall was still down but there were some poles and tape laid beside it. We hopped over into the field and followed our human down to the main gate where we were often fed. A few other humans were there and while we were passed our feed, they hurried up to the gap, pushing the poles into the ground and stringing the tape between then to close it.

Nana scolded us all for our escapades and warned us not to touch the tape. It was, she said, an electric fence to keep us in and would give us a shock if we touched it. I followed her advice, but Erin did touch the tape and confirmed that it 'bit her'.

The sheep returned too, the following day, but they were placed in a different field. Shortly after, a few humans stopped by our field too and put a post and wire fence up inside the stone wall boundary, just in case it fell again and we attempted another outing.

I think if we had had the chance we would have too. The beach had been amazing fun, and I know I wasn't the only one who would go up and stare at the cove longingly after that day.

I wondered if I'd be able to return to the beach one day. I hoped so.

Chapter 3

We spent two idyllic years of our lives in that field together, but none of us ever got back to the beach. I'd often talk with Erin about it, remembering the sounds of the waves up close and how soft the sand was. The others would join in. I remember Shem saying about how good it felt to roll in the sand.

Nana would often take us to the ridge at the top of the field so we could look out at the Galway countryside all around us. She would tell us stories of the beach and the waves that broke on the sand, gently when the weather was calm and thrashing and wild when it was stormy.

She said that some of our ancestors had come from the sea. They had crossed it from a land far away called Spain, in a great fleet of ships the humans called an Armada. Only the ships had been tossed around in one of the wild storms and broken apart in the turbulent waters of the coast.

Many of the humans and horses had drowned in that sea, but some, some lucky few, had washed up or swam to shore safely. Nana said that these horses had been taken in by locals and bred with those already there, making us Connemaras the descendants of survivors.

Sometimes I'd stand there alone and stare out at the water imagining what it was like for those horses. Picturing them in the churning water, finally making their way to the shoreline. Their experience of the Atlantic ocean was much different from mine.

While most of our time was our own, free in our field, we did see some people who came to the yard from time to time. We were all nervous of the strangers that would come to the fields to look at our mothers, Nana, and sometimes even us - but Nana would always explain who they were.

Malley was the most nervous. She was the smallest and youngest of us. She would often hide behind me or Delaney, watching as the humans went about their business until she decided it was safe.

One of the humans came regularly. He often had a bunch of tools with him that almost sent us all into a meltdown the first time we saw him, especially when he started propping Nana's hoof up on a metal stand and rubbing her hoof with a metal bar.

"That is the farrier," Nana explained when she returned. "You'll see him, or a human like him often enough through your lives. He'll check your hooves for signs of trouble, trim them and put on shoes if you need them. Not all horses need shoes though."

"What's a shoe?" I remember my friend Shem, a chestnut filly, asking.

"It is a metal plate fitted to your hoof," Nana replied.

"Does it hurt?" she asked.

"It shouldn't if it is put on correctly," Nana replied.

That made me wonder. She said it shouldn't, not that it didn't.

The vet was our next most frequent visitor. He was a cheerful older man in a flat cap and a strange white coat. The vets I came to meet later always seemed to be dressed differently than this first medical practitioner, but they were all equally invested in ensuring we were healthy and fit.

Nana was very fond of the old man. She said he had saved her life, but never did tell us how. Though often when she said it, her eyes would go a little misty, especially when she looked at us all.

I was not so pleased with the man when he produced a little thing with a plunger on it that pricked my neck. This, I learnt, was something called a vaccination. It was given, so he said, to build up my immune system to fight some diseases that are dangerous to us horses.

I got these regularly from then on. I have no doubt they do help to stop you getting sick. But I still dislike the feel of the needle and to this day will always nod my head when they are given. I got something called a microchip too.

But I did like it when he complimented me though.

"Our young Lir here is a fine lad, isn't he," he would say to Jack. "A perfect example of a Connemara pony. Well balanced, confident, great conformation, fabulous movement and a fantastic attitude," he went on, as he patted me.

"Friendly and full of energy."

"Yes, he's a great pony," Jack agreed, giving my neck a gentle rub. "I almost wish he was the one we were keeping."

He glanced at Erin. Erin was different from the rest of us. She belonged to Jack's daughter Amy, a bright, smiling girl who loved all of us and frequently came to fuss over and love us.

Nana said Erin's mother belonged to Amy, but that she would soon outgrow her and so Erin had been bred for her. I didn't understand this at first. I asked Nana to explain and I remember her looking at me a little sadly.

She told me our time together would be short. One day I would grow up and go off with one of the humans to start my life with them.

I was worried by what she said. I didn't want to leave Nana and my friends and be taken away. Why, I asked, was Erin so lucky? Why would she get to stay here with Amy and not me? It was the luck of the draw, Nana said. She looked at me with a little worry on her face. We can only hope our lives are good, she said.

Erin was larger than me, even though her mother was smaller than mine.

I asked Nana about this too and she snorted in amusement at me.

"Erin is only half Connemara," she replied.

"Her father is something else, something bigger, so she is bigger for her young human to ride."

"What about my father?" I remember asking. "What was he?"

"You are a full Connemara," she said.

"Both your father and mother are what they call oversized Connemaras. That's why you are bigger than a lot of the other foals, but smaller than Erin."

I didn't like being smaller than Erin, but I took pride in being 100 percent Connemara. It sounded like it meant something special.

Our days passed by in blissful freedom, or what we thought was freedom, as free as anything ever gets in the world I suppose. We were happy. What more could we ask for really? We had food, we had space to run and do as we pleased, shelter and, if the weather was cold, extra feed was brought to us.

Jack was kind and cheerful, always checking on us and keeping us safe. I look back at him sometimes and realise he was the best sort of human. The kind who tries their best to do what is right for their horses. Maybe they don't get everything right, but they try.

"Nana," I asked one chilly morning when Jack brought out a giant wheelbarrow full of hay for us.

"What do we do for the humans so that they do this for us? They bring us food, trim our hooves and check our health. We must do something in return?"

"We do," she replied. "And if you get a good human you will go to the ends of the earth for them and back again."

"Are there good and bad humans?" I asked.

"There is good and bad in everything," Nana replied. "And in humans there is much good, much bad and much ignorance."

"What does that mean?" I asked her.

She looked at me kindly.

"Hopefully you will be one of the lucky ones and will never find out," she answered me, turning her attention to the pile of hay we had wandered over to.

Chapter 4

Those years in the fields with my mother, Erin, Malley, Shem, Delaney and Nana seemed endless. Summers stretched long and warm, full of dozes in sunshine, lush grass and play. Winters were harder, but we would huddle together for warmth and shelter, nestled in the bottom of the field in the shelter of the blackthorn bushes.

But Nana was right. In reality that time was short. At three years old we began our working lives. I had grown not to need Nana's constant attention, choosing to spend time with the other fillies and geldings playing together.

As we started our training, we often assembled together to discuss what we had learnt. We quickly realised what we liked and what we didn't.

At first, we learnt simple things. How to wear a bridle and bit - though it was merely a strange squishy bar of rubber. I was asked to walk around and around in circles wearing it, but I never really understood why.

Nana huffed. She grumbled on and on about how humans shouldn't be doing this and that when I was so young. I didn't understand the words she used. Lunge, jump, backed.

Lunging was the first word I came to know. One morning I was put into an odd headcollar with three metal rings on the top of the noseband. It was heavier than the bridle and my headcollar, but it wasn't uncomfortable. I found out later that it was called a cavesson. I was brought into the little paddock we trained in.

As I have said, Jack was a kindly man. He did his best for us, but unfortunately his training techniques (as I later discovered), were not the best for a three year old horse whose body was still growing. He clipped a long rope to one of the rings and waved one end of the rope at me. I moved away from it. This seemed to please Jack so I moved again. I eventually realised he wanted me to walk around him in circles. I wasn't sure why I was supposed to do this, but I did.

The circles were small and I found them both boring to do and painful as I started to feel an ache in my muscles. It was uncomfortable but as Nana always told me, I tried my hardest. Jack was pleased. He smiled up at Amy who was sitting on the fence.

"See love, we start them off right, get them trained up a little so they can find nice owners, have a good life, eh?"

"Yes Dad," she smiled back.

The next day I once again found myself in the paddock with the long rope. Only this time the human didn't wave the rope end at me but a long stick with a long thin tail. Nana told me they called it a lunge whip. Jack waved it and I moved away. He kept this going along with a word, 'walk'. Then he waved the stick again and said 'trot'. I didn't understand.

He made a little jump action with the stick and the little snake-like tail made a popping, snapping noise at my heels. I jumped forward, rushing away from the strange sound, my heart racing. This, however, seemed to be what he wanted. I soon learnt that the little snap sound wasn't going to hurt, it meant go faster. I was relieved that I had learnt what he wanted.

Over the next few weeks and months, the circles became faster. I was asked to walk, trot, and canter them. This was hard. I struggled with the speed, feeling off balance, always worried I would stumble or fall. I found it harder to breathe too. My muscles tensed as I tried and tried to find my balance and yet I constantly heard how good it was for me, for us.

The five of us had similar training and we all felt the same. We could do what we were asked, we understood and tried, but it was so hard for us, trying to balance on the small circles. It wasn't the same as balancing when we were running free together. It made our muscles ache and stressed our bones.

Sometimes I tried to look out of the circle, a way to steady myself, but when I did this Jack would pull my head towards him again. I found myself feeling exhausted after even a short amount of the work, trying to bend myself around, balance and do it at the speed requested. Nana said it was all too much. She said that we were too young to be doing all of this, that our bodies hadn't matured enough yet. I agreed with her, although I wasn't sure what matured was, or when it would happen.

Still, I coped with the training a lot better than Erin. She was almost wild in her attempts to get out of it. Nana cautioned me not to behave like that. Worse things, she said, can happen than lunging. I didn't know what that meant at the time, but if I had, I would have had a long talk with Erin. I often wonder what became of her, and if she learnt to partner with a human, or if her behaviour simply meant she was forced to obey.

Although, while Jack was strict and disciplined in his training routine, Amy seemed to instinctively know what to do. Erin may have been wild on the lunge for him, but she would follow that girl around like a puppy on a leash. I hope that they muddled through and made a great team together.

One fine morning I was brought into the paddock to find there was a strange new obstacle in it. I had been prepared for more lunging, but I had neither the long rope nor the cavesson.

I absently wondered why humans needed all these strange gadgets to work with us. Surely, I could have learnt to walk, trot and canter around the human without it. Nana said she had heard stories of horses trained like that, but she wasn't sure if it was really true. I hoped it was for some horse, somewhere. It was not true for me.

I was led over to the obstacle. A long flat pole lay on the ground. I looked at it and snorted, but it didn't move. Jack led me over it. I wasn't sure why, but I obliged him and he was pleased. We did this again in both directions. He then propped the pole up on a pair of small blocks and walked me over it again. This was harder. I had to lift my feet so they didn't knock the pole.

Next, he fetched the lunge whip and had me go over the little raised pole alone. I managed this and I was very pleased with myself. But if I had known what was to come, I wouldn't have been so happy.

Over the course of a few days my obstacle, which I learnt was called a jump, began to get bigger. I found I could no longer step over it but had to jump over. At the same time Jack began to crack his snake-like whip, asking me to go faster as I jumped. At first, I could cope, trotting and sometimes cantering over the small cross or straight poles, but as they rose higher and his whip urged me even faster, I began to feel more and more anxious.

How I hated going into the paddock and seeing that jump! But never more so than on the day my life course would change forever. I was dragged into the paddock and spotted it straight away. A high straight pole stretched between two white jump wings; two other poles had been balanced on the straight as guides to keep me from running out of either side.

It was much bigger than I had jumped before. I felt my heart race.

I looked around for a means to avoid it, but there was none. I tried to back away from it, but Jack and his whip pressed me forwards. When I tried to dance around and tell him I was scared, that I couldn't do it, he snapped the whip.

"Gerr on, you can do that," I almost closed my eyes as I made a dash at the fence, hoping I could make it over. At the last second, I panicked. I couldn't do it, I couldn't make it. It was too big, too fast.

I scrambled at the fence unable to go over and unable to stop. I remember hitting the wood, the pole feeling heavy as I clattered into it. I felt terrified by the weight of it, rearing to one side only to find the guide poles in the way.

My back legs slid from under me as I tried to right myself. I scrabbled out of the tangle of poles and ran. I ran and ran, but there was nowhere to go. I was trapped in the little paddock. Eventually I saw Jack holding his hands up and speaking to me softly, calmly. I rushed to him hoping for some safety.

He spoke soft words and slipped a rope onto my headcollar. It was only then, as I calmed down and he began to lead me to the gate, that I realised my leg hurt. I'd never felt anything like it before. The calmer I got the more it ached and pinched. I limped after Jack.

"Best call the vet," he grumbled. "What was that? Silly fella." He rubbed my nose.

Jim, the vet, looked at my leg, making me walk and stand, picking it up, holding it out. He gave me something that made me feel very calm and sleepy. When I was fully awake again, I found myself with a shaved leg and a new future. Whatever I had done to my leg, Jim said it meant no more training, at least for some time. I was to rest. And so, while the others were saddled and backed, I remained in the field with Nana.

Chapter 5

One fine morning I was brought in with several of
the other young Connemaras. I expected to restart
my training, to go back in the paddock with the whip
and the lunge, or even to be put in a saddle and sat on
like some of the others. But instead we were greeted
by the sight of a large red truck.

We had seen the truck before. Sometimes it took
mares away for a day or so and then brought them
back. Other times one of the ridden horses would be
gone for the day. Nana said they went to show off.
The year before we had watched another field of
young horses go on it, but none of them had come
back.

At first, we were curious about it. But as the
humans began to put the others on, I realised we
were being taken somewhere. All the young horses I
had been brought in with were going to leave. Like
them I knew we wouldn't be coming back. I called
out for Nana and my mother, hearing her answer my
frantic calls, as I was hauled towards the ramp. I
tried to pull away, to run back to Nana, but they

quickly shoved a rope around my backside, pulling on it and cracking the whip. I could hear Erin whinnying loudly for me too. I was pushed and dragged into the lorry, a partition closing on me so I couldn't escape. I caught a glimpse of Nana through it, a final look at her before Delaney was forced in beside me and the ramp closed, blocking her out along with the light.

The lorry lurched as it trundled along, all of us struggling to stay upright with the strange swaying motion. The lorry smelt odd, a combination of stale straw, previous occupants, acrid fumes, and our own scent. Sweat ran down my body as I tried to stay calm and upright. From either side I heard the heavy breathing of two of my field mates. None of us knew where we were going, or why. Had we known the truth, we may have tried harder not to go into the lorry.

We were unloaded and stuck in little pens with straw on the floor. There were lots of other Connemaras there too. Most of us were a similar age, equally terrified and lost. Some shut down completely, trying to huddle as far away from things as possible, pushing themselves into the corners of the pens, their heads low. They looked small and frozen. Others, like myself, took comfort from the fact we weren't alone, huddling together and wondering what was happening, all equally confused.

The sales are an awful place for horses, especially when you are new to them. Crowded, loud and full of strange smells, sights, and sounds. For someone who has only ever known life in an open field, the sales were a most terrifying place. It assaulted every sense I had and overwhelmed me immensely. I felt suddenly like I knew what those Spanish ancestors of mine had gone through when they had tumbled into the stormy seas from their wrecked ships, abandoned to sink and die or swim to safety on the shore.

I quickly discovered most of the horses I was with had been backed and ridden, though they were my age. It somehow seemed wrong. I was three and I was uncertain of my own balance, let alone the ability to balance a human too. Would the fact I couldn't carry a human yet be bad in this place, I wondered.

Soon people began to wander by the pens. They would stop and look at us, consulting little blue books they held in their hands. I came to understand these blue books told the humans about us, saying things like our age and if we had already been backed. 'Broken and brought on slowly' was a common phrase it seemed. I wasn't sure why anyone would want to break something, and it seemed contradictory to break it and then bring it on. Some of the humans looked us over with hard eyes. I wasn't sure why, but I didn't like the looks they gave us.

A woman came by after a while. She looked kind and had black hair with some grey flecks through it. It strangely reminded me of Nana, with her grey flecked muzzle. She looked about the same age as Jack. Unlike the others, she seemed less interested in the paper and more interested in us.

She came up to each pen, talking calmly with a soothing voice. Still, some of the horses wouldn't move, but I decided I liked her voice. She clicked at me softly and I took a step towards her. She smiled and I came closer still. She rubbed my forehead and scratched my withers. It was a nice relief. A moment of comfort and calm in a chaotic atmosphere.

She spoke to a man who stood beside her with the catalogue. He flicked through it and read a section aloud.

"Lir. 3 years. Full, oversized Connemara, grey," he said. "Erm, unbacked, injury to foreleg, now healed, good breeding."

"He sounds great," the lady smiled at me.

"If you say so Lucy, you're the expert," he smiled at her and patted my neck. "Good boy."

They left and it made me sad to watch them go. But then people came to take us out one by one. I watched as the others were led away to somewhere unseen. As each one left, I began to feel more and more nervous. Where did they go? What did they do? What was expected of me? And what happened after?

I wanted Nana and called out, but there was no answer. Other horses called out too, looking for someone familiar, someone to reassure them.

Finally, it was my turn. I was brought out of the little pen and led towards a gateway. I shrank into myself, terrified of what was happening all around me. Confused and scared, I inched forward. The gate was pulled open and I was led into a little sandy arena. People sat all around me on chairs. A sea of strange faces. I looked around them, some stern, some smiling.

The human leading me began to walk me around the ring one way and then the other, trotting me next and making me do the things I had done on the lunge line in the paddock. I wanted to look at the people, but when I did, I felt I'd overbalance and fall.

Memories of the fence and the poles and the pain flooded back and I tried to focus on my feet.

"Lot 107, 3 years old, grey unbacked oversized Connemara, to make 15.2hh. Who will start the bidding?"

The announcer droned on and on as I paraded around trying to stay upright and breathe. It felt endless, as if I were there for hours. Eventually there was a hammer strike.

"Sold," the announcer said.

I wasn't sure what had just happened. But when I looked up, I saw the friendly woman from earlier smiling at me and hugging the man beside her. As I was taken out of the ring, she was waiting for me. She smiled, taking the rope from the man who had led me around. She patted and stroked me. I looked at her, knowing the fear probably showed on my face, if she chose to see it.

"Hello Lir. It's all going to be alright," she soothed. "You'll be alright."

I didn't know it then, but these two were to be my first real humans, the first ones I would call my own, and it would be Lucy who would show me how horses should really be taken care of.

Chapter 6

My new home was a busy village not far from Limerick, at least that is what my new field mate told me. Dougal was the first Shetland pony I had ever met. He was a small, stocky bay pony who knew, it seemed at the time, everything.

When I arrived shaking and scared, he immediately started to help me settle in. He showed me around our large paddock, the apple tree that hung over one of the stone walls between us and the churchyard next door. He brought me over to the field shelter we had, and told me who lived in the array of little stone houses we could see.

There were two stables, he explained, in a neat little yard behind the shelter, but they were rarely used unless the weather was very bad or there was an injury. To that end he told me never to try and scramble over the wall into the church. I had no intention of doing so, but his warning removed any doubt I may have had. We used the yard mostly for grooming, being cooled off on hot days and for farrier, dentist and vet visits.

Dougal explained that I was, in fact, very lucky. Our human Lucy, he said, was very kind, gentle and above all, very knowledgeable. She had adopted Dougal from her husband's aged aunt. But she longed to be able to ride again, and so had found me. He said not to worry though. Everything I thought I knew about riding and backing would be very different with Lucy. This made me feel much better and I found myself keen to know more. I asked him what he meant, but he said I should wait and see.

We had a great many visitors to the paddock. Every day a parade of small children would appear to brush, pet, and sometimes ride on Dougal, if he had a mind to be caught that is! I decided I loved the children and would always let them catch me. They were young and keen and I saw myself in them. They often brought us treats, though Lucy would insist they put them in rubber buckets for us to have after we had 'worked'. Sometimes they would tickle and scratch me over the fence. I would stand for as long as they chose to be there, bathing in the attention.

Lucy would often show the children how to do things with Dougal, and after I arrived, with me too. She would show them how a hoof pick worked and how to do something called groundwork. I wasn't sure what it was at first. My only training had been lunging and the horrible loose jumping, but Dougal was right, Lucy's training was different.

She would often take us for walks around the village to see things. Sometimes I would go with Dougal, especially if something 'new' or 'scary' had appeared.

One morning I remember seeing workmen for the first time, with their high-vis vests, vans, coils of blue pipe and traffic lights. Lucy assured me these were all fine, but I was still glad that Dougal was there and wasn't worried by it all. She let me watch them for a while, so I could understand they meant no harm. The next morning when I walked past them I barely gave them a second thought. I soon learnt that Lucy was training me, but in my own time.

We often worked in the paddock with the children crowding around to watch too. Lucy would demonstrate what to do with Dougal.

The first time this happened, Lucy put Dougal in a rope halter and walked away with him walking beside her, shoulder to shoulder. When she stopped, he stopped. When she turned, he mirrored her. She then produced a small stick. At first, I was afraid after my encounter with the whip when jumping, but Dougal stood while Lucy ran it all over him. She then touched him very gently, just behind where the girth would sit, and said 'over'. He swung his hind quarters to the rapturous applause of the children and was given a scratch.

Then it was my turn. Lucy put me in the halter and we walked around, me trying to follow her. Sometimes I would get too close and she would look at me, stand up taller and slowly raise an arm into the air as if to make herself look bigger. I'd put my head up in surprise and back away from her, but I quickly learned this meant I was just too close, not that she was going to hurt me.

When she stopped walking, I learned to stop walking too. When she started walking, I did too. It felt like we were connected, walking shoulder to shoulder together. Then she began touching me gently with the stick and I became less afraid of that too.

After our training I would be left alone in the paddock with Dougal. I liked this. It gave me time to be me and to think about what we had been doing and make sense of it. Dougal would explain things too. That was helpful, especially with the long lines.

These were two long ropes that attached to my bridle and passed down my sides through a roller around the space where a saddle would sit. Lucy would then follow behind me using the long ropes to guide where I should go. The signals were confusing at the start, but I figured them out quickly as I knew the words she was saying from our groundwork. Dougal said it was a great way for me to see things without needing him or Lucy right beside me, since he might not be with me on a ride and Lucy would be on my back. I understood that and so tried my best when we went for walks that way.

The groundwork and walks became our daily play. Lucy took me through woods, over little streams and past smells and sights that I had never known existed. Some were beautiful and some were scary, but I began to realise I was safe with her. It made me feel brave and bold, like I could do anything so long as I could hear the calm, steady tone of her voice. If she wasn't afraid, I didn't need to be either.

In the paddock Lucy began to teach me about moving my hindquarters and shoulders using only the rope halter and her voice. I had already learned to follow the feel of the lead rope when it was slack.

Sometimes she would touch the part of my body she wanted me to move, and sometimes, if I was already walking, she would lift the lead rope at just the right moment to ask one of my feet to step sideways a little as it was just leaving the ground. She had really good timing so that really helped me to feel that I was in balance. Dougal said this would be very useful later as I would be able to manoeuvre around better when opening and closing gates while being ridden.

I learned to back up too. This would also be useful when I was out hacking around, Dougal said. Dougal really seemed to know a lot! When Lucy began asking me to move over, she would first gently touch my shoulder to move my front legs sideways, and then touch behind my girth to move my hind legs sideways. Then she would wait a few moments patiently, while I figured it out. She was never in a hurry. But eventually, as I understood more of what she was asking I, just like Dougal, could do it with only one touch at the girth area. I was very proud the first day I did it that way.

"When you teach a horse, you're not making them do something," Lucy would say to the children. "You are actually helping your horse to do something."

The fact that Lucy asked and encouraged made a huge difference in my world. My only sorrow that I couldn't tell my Nana that I was safe and in good hands. I wondered sometimes about my old field mates. Where were they? Did they have a Lucy?

Lucy gave me something else other than the training I would have liked to tell Nana about. She gave me a stable name, at least the first one I ever had.

"Oisin Lir's Storm," she had read from my passport. I flicked my ears at her. "Well, I think we should call you Lir then. God of the sea, a special name for a special horse."

One morning Lucy brought me over to a wooden block that sat in the yard. She called it a mounting block. She had me stand beside it and wait a few moments. When I moved forward, she asked me to go back and I did. Then Lucy praised me and we went for our usual walk. This happened for several days until one morning she climbed onto the block. I tried to look up at her puzzled, but she asked me to step over. Remembering what I was taught, I did this. Lucy bent down and scratched my withers. I loved it so much – sheer bliss!

Withers are a spot you can never reach on your own, and no roll is as good at getting rid of any itches there as a nice scratch. I'd have stood there forever letting her scratch there. Soon enough though we were off on our walk. It was only later I came to realise she had taught me to stand at a mounting block.

Chapter 7

I spent a long time 'playing' with Lucy, that's what she called our training. She said training should be fun for both of us. I liked that. Our walks were the highlights of my week. I began to love going out and seeing new things. I saw huge tractors, ducks that jumped out of bushes unexpectedly and humans going very fast on strange two wheeled things that made no noise. Lucy kept up with our work on the ground too and practising our standing at the mounting block. Dougal told me that all my 'playtime' would be invaluable later.

"Why?" I remember asking him one morning as we watched the mist hanging over the village slowly burn away.

"Because, the signals you are learning now with Lucy on the ground are the same ones she will use when you are ridden. Since you know how they feel already it will be much easier to understand what she wants." I must have looked a little confused because he went on with a small snort.

"Look, most people talk about breaking horses, but we don't want to be broken. We just don't understand what the humans want at first. It's like a human not knowing a foreign language but being asked to talk with a stranger in it, with no help or understanding of the words. Lucy's groundwork lessons are her teaching you the first basic words of a language that you will add to as you go. It makes starting to ride less stressful for you." It strangely made sense to me, although I still wasn't exactly sure what he meant.

I was to find out one fine morning in the spring time when Lucy came out with my bridle. Well, really it looked more like a halter with reins on it. There was no bit, at least not yet. She put it on me and took me to the mounting block as always. I stood and waited for my scratches. She gave me them, and, while I was standing there, she gently lifted her leg over my side and slid onto my back. I stood there, feeling her weight, she wasn't nearly as heavy as I had expected. I shuffled myself a little to adjust to our combined weight and then stood while she praised me and gave more scratches.

She asked me to walk a few steps using signals from our ground work. A small pressure by the girth area and "walk on" was all I needed. I knew this, I had learnt it already. I moved forwards feeling strange with her weight, but not uncomfortable. I wondered how I would feel if someone had simply leapt on me with no preparation at all. I realised I'd have been terrified and confused. It was then I understood what Dougal had meant.

Lucy had soft, gentle hands and took our riding adventure as slowly and deliberately as our in-hand playtime. She was bareback in the beginning, so to start with we stuck to walking around our field with Dougal in tow.

Lucy continued our groundwork lessons and walks continued too. She said it was important and shouldn't simply stop just because we could ride. One thing did confuse me though, in all my training Lucy didn't ever lunge. I only found out why by chance.

We had been doing some in-hand work in the paddock when Jilly came by. She was one of the young girls from the village. She seemed upset and Lucy gave her a hug. I wandered over to see what was wrong. I liked Jilly. She often came to ride Dougal and to brush us. I listened to her explain how she had seen someone at the local stables lunging their young horse for ages before daring to get on. It had upset her because the horse had seemed so frantic.

"Lir isn't like that," Jilly said looking at me with wide eyed innocence.

"But he isn't lunged either," Lucy reassured her. "All the training I do with Lir helps him understand, and when we understand we aren't so scared. Lunging circles puts a lot of stress on a young horse's growing joints and muscles."

"I wish all horses were trained like that," Jilly said, glancing at Dougal and I. I couldn't help but agree wholeheartedly with her.

As our ridden work became a larger part of my life, Lucy began putting an old saddle on me with a thick pad to get used to the feel of it, though she never rode in it. Eventually, she had someone called a saddle fitter come by to check my saddle before she rode me in it.

His name was Philip. He was a kind man with a jolly face who arrived with a lot of saddles in the back of his car. He said my current saddle was a little too long for me. After some discussion and a few false starts with some saddles that were not the right shape, Philip picked out a beautiful second hand mahogany brown saddle and placed it on my back.

"This feels better, doesn't it, fella?" He rubbed my neck making sure I was happy before he gently did up the girth.

Philip spent quite some time making sure the saddle sat on me perfectly. He looked at it from lots of angles, trying to see if any parts of the saddle didn't exactly fit the shape of my back and shoulders. In fact, Philip spent over half an hour checking that that the saddle was the exact width, length and shape for my body. Taking it off, flocking parts and deflocking others.

I was starting to understand that finding a saddle to fit me was quite an in-depth process!

"You'd be amazed," he said to Lucy, as he pulled some fluffy stuff from the front end of the saddle, "just how many saddles I see that are too long for the horse, or are too narrow or wide." He shook his head. "The rider ends up out of balance and the horse ends up with a sore back."

He picked the saddle up and placed it back on me again. It felt different now he had altered it, but in a good way. He did the girth up again.

"Right, let's see you in the saddle," he smiled at Lucy.

Lucy mounted up, giving me time to settle before we both walked a few circles around the field together. Philip walked beside us at one point, slipping his hand between the front of the saddle and my shoulder to check the fit.

"If it pinches me," he explained to Lucy, "it'll pinch him." He smiled. "Looking good."

After a few minutes of walking with Lucy, we stopped and Philip again he checked all over the saddle again as I waited patiently.

Philip checked the saddle over again when Lucy dismounted before finally stepping back with a nod of approval.

"It's a great fit, but he'll change shape fast, youngsters always do. They tone up and they grow. I'd recommend I pop back every three months to give it a once over."

"Whatever's best for Lir," Lucy smiled, patting my neck.

"Grand," Philip smiled. "I'll put it in the diary." He patted my neck. "What a good fella, see, now we have a nice comfy saddle."

He looked over at Lucy. "He's been super given his age, very patient, a credit to you."

Lucy smiled proudly and I stood a little taller. I decided I liked Philip a lot.

The saddle helped distribute Lucy's weight more evenly, but it did dull the feel of her movements a little. After feeling her bareback and then being used to the other saddle, it took some time to adjust to this saddle. But Lucy, as always, was patient with me. The signals she gave were always the same so I wasn't confused.

We continued riding in the field at first, but as we grew in confidence together and I became used to the saddle, we began to take rides along the routes we were familiar walking. Down the lane, passed the green and the pub and church.

I was never scared. I'd seen all these placed before, and if I was lucky some of Lucy's friends would be in their gardens and we'd stop and chat for a while. She'd fuss over me as I stood while she talked, and, if I was very lucky, I'd receive an apple or carrot too. I was especially fond of one of Lucy's friends, a nice old lady with roses around her gateway. Lucy said she was a gardener, but I thought she was a magician, because whenever we came by, she would produce a carrot from her apron pocket for me, without fail.

Eventually, Lucy said we were ready to go a little further, and a little faster. I liked that. We began trying trot and little canters in the field and our walks out grew longer. Soon enough Lucy felt ready to take me to her 'favourite place', the woods. She'd talked to me about it for a long time, describing the trees and the meadows, so I was very excited to see it for myself. The first time I did, I knew instantly it would become one of my favourite rides too!

Lucy loved the woods. In the summer the sun filtered down through the tree branches onto the wide trail that wound through the woods. I could nibble the branches too, if I got the chance. We often went to the woods. I loved how they changed from summer to autumn to winter. It felt like a different place each season.

Lucy not only bought me a saddle, but a bridle too and set about finding me a bit.

Most humans think all horses need a bit. It isn't true. Some of us are happier without one, but if we are ridden in one, finding the right one is more important than they could imagine.

I have had several bits in my lifetime. Some were fitted and were comfortable. Others were not so kind. Lucy took great care when fitting my first bit. She inspected my mouth, running her fingers over the bars of my mouth to see if I needed a straight or jointed bit. She also checked my tongue size and shape and the space there was in my mouth. Finally, after some trials, we settled on something Lucy called a straight bar eggbutt snaffle. It rested mainly on my tongue, not on my bars. It didn't hurt inside my mouth or pinch my lips at all.

The commands used, bit or bitless, were completely familiar to me now and we soon began to work on new things. I learnt to trot and not trip over my own feet while balancing myself and Lucy. We started off in straight lines only, but it didn't take long for us to be able to trot a big circle in the paddock too. Dougal said when I was better at it, I'd be able to trot a really small circle too. He showed me how, prancing around the field, tossing his head.

Canter opened up another world of speed. It made me feel springy and full of energy, like when I was a colt out in the fields with my friends. I liked it very much, especially when I was allowed to canter up the big hill on our outings. It wasn't very steep, but it had a lovely view over the village at the top and I loved rushing up it, the breeze tugging at my mane. I'll admit to sometimes dancing a little with anticipation when we'd get there and feel disappointed if Lucy asked me to walk or trot instead.

In the paddock Lucy began teaching me other things too. We started with moving my hindquarters, just as we had in-hand. I took to this quickly, and soon she added in moving my hindquarters while I was walking, so my hindquarters could do a step or two of a bigger circle than my forequarters, or leg yields moving to the side rather than straight.

I felt immensely proud of myself throughout this training. Sometimes I felt as if Lucy could read my mind, understand what I needed from her to be able to do the things she asked of me. I started to wonder if this was actually the way most humans did train. Maybe my mother and Nana had been unfortunate. I think I knew this wasn't true. Dougal was fond of reminding me how lucky we were. But I was soon to find out first hand just how different humans can be.

Chapter 8

I never thought my time with Lucy would end. It seemed I'd found my place in the world and I was happy with it. Dougal and I got along well. I had everything I needed to be safe and happy, and Lucy was beyond fair and attentive to us both.

Things began to change for us, Dougal, and I, slowly at first. Lucy began to ride less. That was the first thing I noticed. Our play-training became shorter, our outings less frequent. I didn't understand why, but I hoped it would be short lived and we'd soon be back to our former routine. That wasn't to be the case though.

One morning I watched her coming towards the field and I called to her, rushing over eager to go out and see the world. I stopped though, watching as she seemed to struggle carrying our little buckets of feed to the field. I knew they weren't heavy and wondered why she was having so much difficulty. I reached the gate before her and watched as she hauled the buckets into the field for us, leaning on the gate and a little out of breath. In all our walks, our rides, our training, I didn't think I'd ever seen her look so tired.

I snuffled at her, hoping that maybe my presence would make her feel better somehow. She rubbed my head, but her touch seemed lighter somehow, not as vigorous. She didn't stay very long with us, ensuring we were alright and then heading back to the house. That was the day I knew something serious was going on.

Dougal, who had watched from beside me looked worried as he watched her go. I turned to him hoping he had an answer to what was happening. He did, but I didn't like it.

"I think she's sick," he said.

"What sort of sick?" I asked looking after her. "Didn't she have her vet jabs?"

Dougal gave a little snort. "Not that sort of sick. I've seen humans like this before."

"Well, when will she get better?" I asked. I hoped it would be quickly.

Dougal looked away. "Sometimes they don't," he said as he headed sadly away into the field. I stayed by the gate staring in the direction Lucy had gone.

Sometimes they don't? What did that mean? We couldn't lose Lucy, could we?

I tried my best to be well behaved and put no additional strain on Lucy for the next few weeks, but I could see her weaken as the days ticked by. One morning she didn't come at all. I began to worry and I know Dougal did too. We waited huddled together close to the gate, nibbling at the grass, but neither of us really eating.

Eventually Lucy's husband appeared. He looked pale and tired. He fed us, checked we were alright and then left. I looked at Dougal feeling more and more anxious. We spent a restless day together not sure what was happening. It might have been longer if not for Jilly. She turned up after school with her mother, dumping her little bag on the mounting block and fetching our halters. She picked out our hooves, brushed Dougal and fed us both, while her mother headed inside with something in a pot.

"I know Lucy will want your hooves done," she said with a little sniffle. She hugged Dougal. "She'll be ok, I know she will."

Dougal snuffled at her pockets, snuggling into her. I wished I had someone to snuggle into like that. Somehow, I felt like I needed someone to be close too. Jilly turned Dougal and I loose, picked up her bag and headed off, glancing back over her shoulder as she took her mother's hand and headed along the road.

For the next few weeks that was how things were. Lucy's husband would check on us in the morning, and after school Jilly would come by, brush Dougal and feed us both. Jilly was too small to really groom me, though she often patted me if I lowered my head down to her. I missed my scratches and brushes. My coat began to lose some of its shine, but I didn't care. I missed Lucy and our training. I began to wonder if I would ever leave the paddock again. The thought made me feel sad, but I was to learn there were worse things than never leaving the paddock.

One morning a strange van appeared by the house. I couldn't see it very well, but I could see enough to watch as two men in overalls that resembled the ones the vet wore went into the house. A little while later they brought Lucy out on a little stretcher. I called after her and she turned her head to look at me, and then the men put her into the van, hopped in and it drove away.

A little while later a strange car arrived and a woman got out. She looked like a younger version of Lucy. Dougal shouted when he saw her and trotted across, she glanced in our direction, but headed straight inside.

"Who is that?" I asked.

"That's Clare, Lucy's daughter," Dougal said. "She's grown up and lives miles away."

We took to waiting by the gate again, and soon enough both Lucy's husband and Clare came out to the yard. He began readying our little buckets of chaff and apples.

"I can't keep doing it Clare," he huffed. "I have work."

"I know Dad, but," she glanced in our direction. "It's Mum's life."

"I know love, but, can you take over?"

"You know I would Dad, if I could."

"Then I don't have a choice," he shook his head.

I didn't understand what was going on, but I was to find out quickly. Clare stayed for a little while; it turns out she was as good with horses as her mother. She brushed me and even took me out a few times. She felt different to Lucy, but similar enough and the signals she used were familiar.

She seemed to enjoy our little rides and I wondered if she might take care of me until Lucy came home. A few days later however, several strangers began to come by. They didn't bother with Dougal, but would look me over, asking questions about me and sometimes riding me. I didn't like it.

"What's happening?" I asked Dougal.

He looked at me with sad eyes. "You don't know?" I shook my head. "They're trying to find you a new human, a new home."

I felt my heart sink. They were getting rid of me. Did Lucy know? Did she want me to go? I shook that thought away. I knew Lucy didn't want that. I knew she wanted me, but she wasn't here. That was it wasn't it? She was my human but she couldn't take care of me right now and so I had to go. I felt my heart break. It broke because I wanted to stay. It broke because I knew Lucy wanted me and couldn't have me. Then another thought came into my mind. Where would I go and who with? And what about Dougal?

I looked at him. "What about you?"

At that moment the sound of Jilly's bag hitting the wooden mounting block broke through my thoughts.

I watched her pick up the halter in her tiny hands and stride towards the gate.

"I'll be ok," he said to me as she pulled open the gate.

Chapter 9

I was six years old when I left Dougal, Limerick and Lucy behind for somewhere new. As I climbed the horsebox ramp, I glanced back at the little bay Shetland wishing him the best life. I hoped that Dougal, and perhaps I, would one day see Lucy again. She wasn't there when I left and I felt, as I had with my mother and Nana, both a sense of loss and of heartbreak at not being able to say goodbye.

Jilly and her mother, we had learned, were stepping in to look after Dougal. She was there when I left and I saw her bury her sad little face in Dougal's neck. I wondered absently if she was sad at my leaving, at the fact Lucy was missing it, or if she simply felt bad that Dougal was losing a friend. I decided I hoped it was for me and chose to think it was. She gave the human that loaded me an apple for my dinner.

My new human Alison, owned a show jumping yard. It was large and clean and busy. I'd never been somewhere so noisy. There was a stable yard that most of the horses, myself included, lived in most of the time. I had never spent much time in a stable before, and while I found it comfortable with a deep bed and fresh hay, I missed the freedom of being out in the paddock all day every day.

The horse stabled to my left, I soon learnt, was called Seamus. He was a large piebald showjumper of unknown breeding, who was seemingly very happy with his regimented life. He greeted me with a little whicker when I first arrived and soon began to talk about the yard, how it was run with precision as it should be, and about the other horses on it. He introduced me to his neighbour, on the other side to me, a smaller pony called Hamish, whose human was the yard owners' daughter. He was, he said, half Welsh cob, half Connemara like me, although unlike me he was a bright dun colour.

"Where are you from?" he asked me cheerfully. I must have looked confused because he added. "I mean where were you born?"

"Galway," I replied a little less timidly than I felt.

"Ah, nice part of the world." Seamus cut in. "I was born right here in Dublin myself. Did you know you were in Dublin? Capital of Ireland you know, Dublin."

There was a derisive snort from my right and I looked over to see a chestnut mare glancing in Seamus's direction.

"Ignore him," she said to me shaking her head. "He has no idea what he's talking about. Everyone knows the real capital of Ireland is Cork."

"Now Shannon, just because you were born in Cork..." Seamus started, but she cut him off.

"Young fellow doesn't want to know about Dublin. What's your name?" she asked me kindly.

"Lir," I replied. "It means 'sea' in old Irish."

I expected her to continue our conversation, but at that moment someone came into the barn with a little trolley on wheels piled high with buckets.

"Tea," Hamish stomped his feet excitedly. "About time."

The human with the trolley began to place buckets over our doors. I waited patiently for mine and stepped back politely until it was delivered just as Lucy had taught me. Shannon however glared at the human with the buckets, pinning her ears back and barging at the door until the man clapped his hands at her and chased her away enough to get the bucket over the door. She rushed back as soon as she could and only after the man had stepped away did she go to her feed.

"What was that?" I asked Seamus watching her display in horror.

"Oh, she's just a grumpy sort," he huffed.

"That's not true," Hamish whispered just loud enough for me to hear. "She's just been hurt, that's all."

"Is that true?" I asked. I glanced at Shannon. "I was hurt too. When I was very young, my human asked me to run and jump over a big fence in the paddock, but I couldn't and I slid into it. I hurt my leg."

Hamish shook his head. "It's not that kind of hurt."

"What he means," Shannon said looking up from the bucket. "Is that I refuse to give in to humans. If they are going to treat me roughly and pretend I am an object like a boot rather than a living creature, I am not going to play nicely with them." She held her head up a little haughtily. "If I mean so little to them, why should they mean anything to me?"

"You just don't understand them," Hamish piped up.

"Well, I wish I did, then perhaps I'd know what they wanted. Better yet I wish they could understand me, wouldn't that be something. You know," she glanced at me. "I was once squashed into a tiny lorry. And I mean too tiny. I knew it was too small. How they didn't know I have no idea. I mean I wouldn't have been able to breathe in it. So, I refused to go in. Do you know what they did? They put a rag over my face so I couldn't see, spun me around and beat me with a stick until I rushed forwards and found myself in the stupid thing. I panicked of course, I mean, who wouldn't."

"What happened?" I asked.

"I reared and fell. I cut open my head and jarred my back. Apparently, a lame, injured horse makes them listen. I was on box rest for two weeks, but ever since they've at least had the sense to travel me in the big lorry so I can breathe." She looked indignant. "I'd have thought that my refusing to go in would be enough, but no, they never understand. That's when I learnt, you have to double down in your efforts if you want them to listen to you."

"My human did," I sighed thinking of Lucy. "Understand me I mean. She understood everything."

"And yet, here you are," Shannon pointed out. She looked at me her eyes softening. "Don't get attached to them, they'll only break your heart. Humans don't stick around. They sell you on as if you're a piece of furniture and replace you on a whim."

I looked at her. She seemed sad and disillusioned. I wondered how many humans she had had, but I didn't want to be rude and ask. I thought back to Lucy. Lucy had understood me, and I was pretty sure she hadn't wanted to get rid of me, replace me or anything like what Shannon had said. She was sick, that was all. It wasn't her fault, just as it wasn't mine. I looked over at Seamus and Hamish. The coloured jumper had dozed off, muttering a little and slightly nodding his head.

"Don't let Shannon put you off the humans," Hamish said. "They aren't all bad. My girl, Chloe, she's a good one."

"She's a child," Shannon muttered. "She'll grow up."

"Aye," Hamish nodded. "But I intend her to grow up as a good one. With a little help from me."

I looked from one to the other wondering what my life here would be like. Over the course of my lifetime, I've gone back over that moment thousands of times and I realise that at times I have felt like both Shannon and Hamish.

Chapter 10

My training at the showjumping yard was very different to what Lucy had done with me. I didn't see much of Alison at all. She always seemed very busy doing something. Instead one of her employees, Ryan was in charge of riding and training me. Ryan was younger than Lucy, only in his twenties. He was tall, and thin with short dark hair and smelled of cigarettes. Gone were my walks and all the in-hand work. Instead I found myself usually ridden in the arena. It was repetitive and a little dull. What was worse, while the basic signals Ryan used were the same, his style was very unfamiliar and I struggled to understand him. He used the same words as Lucy, but his hands were harder and he hauled at the bit in my mouth, rather than using his seat and weight to help guide me as Lucy had.

I found myself frequently opening my mouth, trying to avoid the tugging of the bit. This seemed to infuriate Ryan and one day he brought a new bridle for me to work in. At first, it didn't seem too different from my old one, but this had an additional strap that wrapped around my nose under the bit and fastened closed, making it impossible for me to open my mouth at all.

Shannon called it a flash and I hated it with every fibre of my being. The band was tight around my nose and made it hard for me to breathe, especially when we did fast paced work. I often felt like I had to fight for each breath and needed to snatch my head forward from the pulled in position Ryan seemed to want me to work in. This would irritate him, and I longed for him to understand me as Lucy had.

"I don't understand how to do what he wants," I complained to Shannon.

"It wouldn't matter if you did," she huffed. "It wouldn't change anything. He'd still put you in the flash and ride you that way."

"But if I understood, I could do it without the flash," I pointed out. "He could take it off."

She let out a soft chuckle of a wicker. "Oh sweetheart, once they've put you in something they don't take it off! They don't change things back; they get stuck in a pattern of "this is what I need" and stay that way."

I looked at her horrified hoping that wasn't true. I didn't want to spend my life in the flash! The thought made a cold sweat break out all over me. It was the worst thing I had experienced so far in my life. I braced myself every time I saw it, knowing I'd spend the next hour feeling like I couldn't catch my breath. I'd grow more and more anxious and tense through the ride, the feeling of panic rising as my breath became more ragged. It was terrifying, every second feeling like an hour.

Living in the barn posed some problems too. It meant that I couldn't run around as I was used to in the paddock and I soon found myself with a lot of energy every time I was let out. I'd jog on the rope keen to be set free and sometimes I would dash through the gateways spinning around and dancing as I waited excitedly to be released. As soon as I was free, I'd spin and buck with joy, tearing around the field in glee before dropping and rolling. I'd done this once with Lucy, when Dougal and I had been stuck in our stables for a full day and night during a snowstorm. She had understood I was just happy; she'd steadied me and made me walk through the gate again, keeping myself steady, before laughing at my explosion as I pranced in the snow and rolled in it.

I thought, therefore, that the humans would understand this as exuberance, but I quickly learnt to these new humans it meant I was 'highly strung'. Ryan began to refuse to lead me out without something called a chifney. It was like a headcollar with a bit in it that he would yank on every time I jogged or tried to surge at the gateway. It became another thing to bite into my mouth and cause pain, and another example of how little they understood me.

Soon enough I found that between the chifney and Ryan's rough hands when we rode, my mouth felt sore all the time and not just when I had a bit in it. My neck grew stiff and sore too from having my nose pulled into my chest when we trained. After a while, the stiff and soreness seemed to spread through my whole being, to the point I was uncomfortable in the field as well as when we rode.

I wasn't sure how Ryan couldn't tell. I must have moved badly, tense and stiff, but he didn't seem to notice at all. I remembered what Shannon had said, about having to give them the least subtle sign before they would understand something. Was she right? I tried for a few days to tug at the reins and even throw in a little buck to try and show Ryan I was sore, but he seemed to think I had too much energy and cut back my feed.

"Don't worry," Shannon told me as I stared at the chaff in my bucket. "You get used to the pain eventually. It becomes like a buzz in the background of life, you barely notice it."

I glanced at her, feeling utterly defeated. Was this really how life was for us? I snuffled at my feed feeling unenthusiastic, so much so I was 'flat' during my next ride according to Ryan. He simply upped the feed again.

I may have started to feel more and more like Shannon. I might even have become grumpy and snippy with the humans if it hadn't been for three things. Nana's words rang in my head over and over again. Do your best. That's what she had told me to do and I couldn't let her down.

Then there was Lucy. I knew Shannon wasn't right, not every human was deaf to our needs and feelings. I had proof - Lucy. She had listened to me, other humans would too. Perhaps not Ryan, but others. I just had to hope one would come along in my life again, until then I guessed I'd have to put up with it.

The final reason was a small girl. Chloe. She was Hamish's human. She was small and sweet, with long blonde hair and big blue eyes. She would speak to and pat all of us, even Shannon, who surprisingly did not snap at the girl. Chloe was kind and gentle, her little hands soft on my nose when she'd come in to say good morning or goodnight.

I watched her feed Shannon a carrot once, rubbing her nose and snuggling up to her. Ryan caught them and scolded Chloe, telling her off for putting herself in danger by being so close to the mare. I remember Chloe turning to look at him unphased.

"She likes me," she said simply, still patting Shannon.

"She usually bites." Ryan replied. "She bit me."

I watched the girl shrug. "Maybe she just bites people she doesn't like." I got the impression this small force of nature was not so fond of Ryan; it made me like her even more.

Watching Chloe kept the memories of Lucy and Jilly alive for me. Remembering those times in the paddock, the kind training and soft hands were the only things that kept me going and stopped me from being as grumpy with Ryan as Shannon was.

Chapter 11

"The worst thing, in my opinion," Shannon said, leaning out over her door, "are draw reins."

I listened as the others discussed which pieces of equipment the humans used were their least favourite. It was a long list, most of which I hadn't even heard of and I was beginning to dread ever experiencing any of them.

"Yes, quite awful things," Seamus nodded his head.

"What are they? What do they do?" I asked, feeling my heart quicken.

"They're torture devices if you ask me," Shannon huffed, tossing her mane.

"They're leather straps," Hamish said lifting his head from a pile of hay. "Like reins the humans hold, but longer, they thread through the bit and fasten to the girth."

"But, wouldn't that force your head down?" I asked.

"That's the point," Shannon said. "They stop you looking up. Imagine," she shuddered,   "I was once ridden out in them, I heard all the sounds of the world but couldn't look up at them, or find out what they were. It was the most terrifying ride of my life."

"It's cruel, that's what it is," Seamus nodded. "We're prey animals after all. We need to see if danger is coming, and you can't do that with your nose between your knees."

"Not to mention how much they hurt your muscles," I absently heard Shannon add.

I thought about what Seamus had said about danger. When I had trained with Lucy, she had been very particular about me being able to see scary things. I was to stop, look, take my time and only when ready walk past them. I was always allowed to lift my head and look. I would naturally lower my head a little once I was certain that whatever I had seen wasn't going to attack us, and I started to relax.

"Have you all been ridden in them?" I asked.

"Nope," Hamish answered, munching away. "Chloe doesn't like them. She read an article about them in her horse magazine. Apparently, they are the training aid most likely to do harm. She tried to empty the tack room of them all, but her mother saw her and made her stop."

"I sometimes wish I was a pony," Shannon mumbled. "The rest of the time I wonder how it is a child has more sense and compassion than an adult human."

"You know," Seamus put in. "I've heard some humans talk about why they use them."

"They want their horses' body to be in a certain outline and shape, so we can be healthy and athletic, but also sometimes just to impress their friends and do well at competitions - but they have no idea how to teach us to do it.

So instead they buy these awful gadgets and leather straps. But how do we explain that it's not fair on us and they make us sore? It's not like we can just tell them! They never listen to us!" Shannon said, with a deep sigh.

They kept on talking, but I noticed something across the yard. It had started to rain heavily, and a small figure in a mackintosh and red wellingtons was darting through it towards the small stone building that housed the feed and tack rooms, an orange bag tucked under one arm. I wondered what treat Chloe had brought for Hamish today. For a second, I echoed Shannon's thought of wanting to be a pony.

Chloe was only in the feed room for a few seconds before she came running out. Her hood was pulled back and the rain hammered down, soaking her head, and plastering her blonde hair to her cheeks, although she didn't seem to notice. I caught a glimpse of her determined face as she stormed across the yard, her boots slapping in the puddles of water that had pooled in places.

"I wonder what's up with her?" Seamus asked.

"I don't know," I replied poking my nose out over the door. "She was only in there a minute."

"Chloe?" Hamish whickered. She didn't even glance over. Something was going on.

A few seconds later Ryan appeared from the same building looking around, but Chloe was already out of sight. He began to make his way across the yard, but before he could get very far Alison appeared with Chloe beside her. The rain had begun to ease now, the fat drops quickly turning to drizzle.

"So," Alison said tapping her foot and crossing her arms. "It seems we've found out where all those missing things have been going." She glared at the young man standing indignantly in the rain. He looked over at Chloe with a little sneer.

"I'm not sure what you're talking about..."

"Don't even start with that, Chloe saw you Ryan, you're our thief."

Ryan put a hand on his chest. It seemed like he was trying to look innocent, but I could tell with one look at his face he was about to lie.

"I don't think so, she must have seen something wrong." Ryan shook his head. "I was the one who told you stuff had started to go missing in the first place."

"Are you calling my daughter a liar?" Alison asked a dark look spreading across her face.

"No, no, just she saw wrong," Ryan scrabbled.

"Get off my yard," Alison pointed at the gateway. "Now. Get off and don't come back. The rest of your wages will be deducted for whatever you've taken, and don't for one second think about complaining about it or my next phone call will be to the Guards."

"Fine," Ryan stormed. "I don't want to be here anyway." He stomped away, marching past us on the way to his car. I watched him go, secretly hoping I'd never see him again.

"Well," Alison said looking down at Chloe. "I guess I'd better start looking for a new rider and yard hand."

"I can do it," Chloe piped up. "At least, I can feed."

"Thank you." Alison smiled at her before heading inside her house, pulling her phone out as she went.

Chloe marched into the feed room and shortly afterwards came out with the little trolley on wheels, buckets piled up on it. She pushed it along to our stables and began to open the doors, slipping buckets inside. She hugged Hamish as he put his nose in his bucket, petting him and giving him a kiss on the cheek.

When she opened my door and placed my bucket inside, she slipped in too. She looked at me with kind eyes and gave my forehead a rub.

"He's gone now, good riddance, he was awful. Maybe the next rider we get will be better." She smiled at me and stroked my neck.

For a moment I remembered life with Lucy, soft hands stroking my hair. It felt so nice, like I had someone of my own again. Hope flooded through me. Chloe, Lucy, Jilly. There were nice humans out there.

Chapter 12

As it turned out, my new rider and the yard hand were two different people. They arrived soon enough. The yard hand, Meg, was a kindly older teenager that often babysat for Alison, and what she lacked in horse knowledge was made up for by her soft-spoken nature and willingness to learn. We all liked Meg instantly, helped by the fact Chloe loved her.

My new rider was called John. He was older than Ryan by a fair margin, and his experience showed. The very first thing he did was put all of the draw reins in a box that   he shoved on a high shelf in the barn.

"Won't be needing these," he muttered as he pushed it into place. "Will we?" He glanced in our direction. If we could have told him we agreed, we would have.

He next set about getting to know us all. While Meg was the yard hand, John liked to pitch in as he called it. He often turned us out. He took one look at the chifney, tossed it in the box with the draw reins and found me a headcollar that fitted. I pricked my ears up and nuzzled him, hoping he understood how much I appreciated this.

"Didn't like it, hey?" He patted me and ruffled my forehead. "Well then, let's behave ourselves shall we and we won't need it." He pulled a face, scrutinising me. "Chifney hhmm. Right, let's be seeing in your mouth young fella."

He opened my mouth a little and I stuck my tongue out a little, the feeling unfamiliar and strange. He sniffed as he examined my mouth, taking an interest in the areas that hurt the most. How had he known?

"We'll need something for that," he nodded. I wasn't sure what he meant, but I was happy he had noticed there was a problem.

He took me out of my stable and I tried my best to walk with him, I really did. I did jog a little beside him when we were close to the paddocks, bouncing upwards rather than pulling.

"Now, now," he said, "Steady on, I don't walk that fast lad," but he smiled as he said it, and didn't yank on the rope. I settled at the sound of his voice and he patted me.

That evening when I came in Alison and Chloe were waiting. John showed them my mouth. "You see that? That's hard hands and a chifney for you, look at how cracked and dry the corner of his mouth is." He pulled out a jar and smeared some white cream on my sore mouth. It felt instantly better and I think I let out a sigh.

"See," Chloe squeaked beside Alison. "Ryan was awful." She smiled at John.

"We'll give him a few days before I ride, and let that mouth heal up a bit. I'll take a look at his tack though."

"I'll fetch it," Chloe beamed and rushed off.

I decided that like Chloe, I liked John. I had hope that perhaps, just perhaps my life was going to turn in a positive direction.

"Huumm," Shannon watched as John put the lid back on his pot of mouth cream. "Well, he's better than the last one. We shall see."

"Does that mean you won't bite him?" Seamus asked.

She glared at him. "I said, we shall see."

The first thing John did when looking at my tack was pull off the flash noseband. He located a nice, wide, padded cavesson and put it on instead. I felt my heart soar. My mouth was being treated and the chifney and flash had gone. I felt as though a weight had been lifted from me that I hadn't realised was there. I finally understood what Shannon had meant about discomfort becoming a background buzz. That is what had happened to me, but now that it was being corrected, I felt lighter and happier.

In the end it took two weeks for my mouth to have healed enough for John's liking. He started long lining me in a headcollar before then though. I think I surprised him at how easily I took to it. He had no idea about Lucy of course, and all the things she had taught me.

When we did start to ride together, I found him far different to Ryan. Gone was the fast pace, the rushing, and the heavy hands. There was no being tugged into fences, no feeling that I couldn't breathe. John rode with much lighter hands, though admittedly not as light as Lucy's had been. Without the flash I felt I could stretch and relax and because I could breathe freely, I could concentrate on what John was asking me, rather than desperately just trying to get to the end of the ride.

John took things slowly, teaching me what he wanted by repeating things. If I went over a jump too quickly one time, he'd steady me more the next. If I was too slow, he'd ask me to go on a little faster, although never beyond my comfort level. I soon grew to understand what pace was needed for what fence, how many strides I'd need and how tight I could cut a corner without feeling unbalanced. I began to quite enjoy popping over the little fences John would put up for us. It was like flying, and I found I was good at it. It reminded me of that day when we all escaped to the beach and jumped through the waves when I was younger, dancing in the sunlight.

I found myself hacking once again too. Whereas a hack with Ryan had been a fast blast around a field and home, John let us take our time. I could see things again, fields, trees, the world outside the yard gates. I liked it. Often, I had company too. Sometimes it was Seamus, sometimes Chloe and Hamish. I loved the hacks with Hamish, he was always happy to wander along, but then to whizz up his and Chloe's favourite hill. John would always hold me back a little so Hamish won and Chloe would beam and say he was the fastest pony in the world. He'd look so proud and snort and stamp a foot.

Life was good. I even had chance to go to my very first competition. It wasn't far from the yard and there was a little debate about hacking there, but in the end, we took the lorry I had arrived on. It was much nicer going into it with Hamish, all plaited up knowing we'd come home in the evening, than it had been the day I left Lucy's.

The little show was fun. It was busy with lots of new things to see and horses to meet. Hamish of course had done all this before. He talked me through things.

"That's the ridden ring," he said poking his nose at a line of horses parading around. "There's the jumping." I glanced over at a little fenced off bit of ground with painted poles and white wings. "That'll be you I reckon. Last off there's the games, that's the best."

He was right. The little jumps were for John and I. We went around twice in the end. I tried not to be too distracted by everything going on around us while we jumped, which was hard. I must have done alright because John praised me a lot and even gave me an apple when he ate a sandwich and drank a coffee he got from a strange looking van.

We came home with four ribbons between us. Three for Hamish and Chloe, one for a ridden class and two for pony games. My ribbon was yellow and had a 3 on it. Hamish said that was a very good thing for my first time out. It wouldn't be my last or even highest placed rosette, but I think it's the one I'm most proud of.

Chapter 13

Not too long after our show, a large lorry arrived and out of it stepped King. King was a showjumper who competed most weekends. His owner, Thomas, introduced himself to John and Meg.

"Oh, he's fine to handle. He is a pain to tack up, but he loves to jump," Thomas chuckled.

We all stared at the large bay horse, eager to meet him. He was put in the isolation box around the corner from us for a few days, since he had just come from a large competition yard and Alison wanted to make sure he had no infections he could pass to us before we met. It was hard to tell much about him for the first few days.

I watched him jump a few times in the school from my paddock. True enough, he would hurl himself at the fences jumping far above what he needed too, but I wasn't sure it was out of joy. When I jumped with John, I felt like I was flying. When King jumped, he looked like he had sat on the electric fence. It was as if he expected the jumps themselves to come alive and bite him. It confused me, but I was soon to learn just how King felt about jumps and why.

King moved into our barn a few days after I had seen him jumping. He came in snorting and prancing about on the lead rope. Thomas simply whacked his chest with the rope and then shoved him into the stable. He darted back over the door staring around himself a little wild eyed.

"Oh no," Shannon sighed. "Not another stressed gelding."

"Hello," I said. "My name is Lir. I jump too."

King looked at me as if seeing me for the first time. He almost shuddered at the word jump. "I don't like to jump."

"Humans seem to think you do," Seamus pointed out.

"I don't!" King huffed.

"Why not?" I asked.

King seemed to regard me for a moment. He sighed and let out a breath. He suddenly seemed a little less tense. "Because of the poles. The poles, they jump up and hit you."

"Are you talking about rapping?" Seamus asked. King looked at him as if he were confused. "The poles, instead of staying still, they moved upwards and hit your legs?"

"Yes. Do they do that here too?" King asked tensing again.

"No," Seamus shook his head. "No they stay still."

I looked over at Seamus confused. "What does he mean?"

Seamus sighed. "Some people use a technique called rapping to make horses jump bigger. They do it to get the horse to pick its feet up more, so they don't knock a pole or get faults at competition."

"But what is rapping?" I asked.

"People will hold a pole and lift it as the horse jumps over, hitting their legs with it, so the horse learns that it must jump far above the pole in order to not be hurt," Seamus explained.

I glanced at King. "That's awful! That happened to King?"

"So, it would seem. Although I think he believes it was the poles that moved, rather than a human moving them."

"Humans," Shannon huffed. "Hitting horses with poles so they get extra ribbons at meaningless shows."

King never really seemed calm. There was always an air of tension about him, as if he were unable to relax. Even loose in the field he was prone to spooking. The worst thing for him though seemed to be his saddle. Whenever he saw it, his muscles clamped. He'd dart about as Thomas tried to put it on, to the point he would need to be tied outside so there was room for Thomas to leap away if King lashed out. I watched this in confusion. Lucy of course had introduced me to saddles properly. The one Lucy had put me in had been fitted to me carefully, and even now was regularly checked and altered by the nice saddle man who came to visit a couple of times a year. I couldn't understand why King hated it so much.

One day while we were in the barn alone with just Shannon, cooling down after a hack, I asked King about his hatred for tack. He looked at me as if I was strange.

"Well," he said. "From the stable. From when it's first put on. How can you be calm remembering how it's done the first time?"

I was confused. "The first time, well, it felt a little odd I suppose," I agreed. "But Lucy did the girth up slowly and we only walked around side by side for a few minutes, then she took it off. I think I got used to it pretty quickly after that."

"What about when you had it on in the stable?" King asked.

"I didn't really have it on in there much," I admitted. "Some very cold mornings when we went out for a hack Lucy would tack up in there after she groomed."

"No, I mean when they put the saddle on and shoved you into the stable in the dark, overnight so you could get used to it."

I looked at him horrified. "Is that how you learnt to wear a saddle?" I asked.

"Isn't that how it's always done?" King replied.

I looked at Shannon. "No dear," the chestnut mare put in with a sigh. "Some humans are better at these things than others." I was surprised at that. I looked at her and saw pity in her face.

"I won't trust humans after that, or their saddles and poles." King huffed.

"Is that why you won't be caught?" I asked, remembering how long Thomas had spent trying to retrieve King after Meg had accidentally turned him out without his usual field headcollar.

"I don't want them near me, none of them," he replied.

I thought about all the times I'd seen him bite and kick out at people. Shannon would scowl, but as far as I knew she'd only ever actually bitten Ryan. King would let fly at anyone. Even Chloe gave him a wide berth, somehow seeming to sense he wasn't to be trusted. Hamish had gone so far as to warn him to stay away from her.

"All humans do is hurt you," King huffed breaking through my thoughts. "Especially with the saddles. That girth, it hurts so much inside when it's fastened up. I'm not sure how you bear it without biting them. There is so much pain in my stomach and sides every time it's done up and I'm ridden."

"Oh," Shannon looked out over the door. "I've heard of that before. King my dear, you likely have an ulcer, that's what causes the pain in your stomach. Eat something before you ride, it helps a lot. You should make sure you have hay in your stomach before you go out too, young Lir. It can help ulcers stop forming in the first place."

I took Shannon's words to heart and have eaten several handfuls of hay at least before every ride I could. It was good advice and served me well over the years. King however, simply turned away from her, reluctant to even try. I think he was just too tense when he knew a ride was imminent to even attempt to eat.

Chapter 14

As well as shows, we occasionally went on other outings together. Alison would load up the lorry and drive us to places for longer hacks and rides. We visited the forest often, but I remember the first time best of all.

Hamish was the most excited for the ride. He loved zooming around the little trail with Chloe, hopping over fallen logs, but he also loved to tell us spooky stories about the place too. I never paid much heed to his tales of fairy rings and spirits lurking in the woods. Shannon said it was silly nonsense, but King believed everything.

"Sometimes the spirits will lead you along the wrong path," Hamish said. "Make you lose your way. There's one tree, a big gnarled one beside a gate that is haunted by the spirit of a lost horse, doomed to be trapped in the woods forever."

King shuddered and Seamus looked up from his hay with a sigh. "Do us a favour Hamish, put your hoof in your mouth there's a good fellow, some of us would like to sleep tonight and you are frightening poor King."

"He is not!" King huffed, but the whites of his eyes were showing just a little.

I snuggled down into my bed excited for the next morning. I'd been on several little rides with Shannon and Hamish, but this was only my second outing with John, and I was looking forward to it.

The woodland ride was divided into several routes, each taking longer than the previous. We parked up in a little car park surrounded by trees and stepped out to the smell of pine and damp earth. It was a dry, if a little grey morning. We were to ride together for a while and then split up; Hamish, Chloe, Shannon and Alison taking a shorter circuit back to the lorry, King, Thomas, John and I doing the middle loop which was longer and a little too tricky for Chloe.

Our ride started well. We ambled along chatting to one and other and enjoying the fresh scent of the woods. Even King seemed a little less tense than usual although Shannon put that down to the fact there were no poles to attack him and because he had eaten something on her instruction while we travelled.

We cantered along some of the trail, the soft pine needle floor thudding under my hooves. It felt soft and springy. I liked the feeling a lot. Eventually we made it to a field where there was a fork in the trail. One way passed through a gate into a wide open meadow-like paddock that you crossed before rejoining the woods. The other curved around the field before swinging back towards the lorry.

"I suppose we shall see you back at the lorry shortly," Shannon said, glancing along the trail that continued in the woods.

"Sure, so long as the fairies don't get them," Hamish joked.

I rolled my eyes at him as they headed away and waited while John opened the gate so we could enter the field. The meadow field sloped upwards so that we couldn't really see much of the top of it. John suggested we trot it, although Thomas had been keen to go faster. It turned out that John made a very good decision, because as we neared the top of the field, where it re-joined the woods, we saw something that alarmed me and terrified King.

The gateway back into the woods was guarded by an enormous, gnarled old oak tree. Its knotty bark cast in dark shadow even in the grey hues of the day.

Wrapped in its branches were shreds of something black that flapped and twisted in the wind, like long fingers reaching out towards us.

Beneath both the tree and the gate was a large pool of water. From the position we were in, with the light as it was, the pool looked inky black. It could have been deep enough to swallow us whole, or barely reach half way up a hoof, it was impossible to tell. I stopped dead in my tracks and stared just as Lucy had told me to. King stopped too.

"It's the tree from Hamish's tale, isn't it?" King shuddered. He backed away from the gate. Thomas immediately growled at him and yelled, kicking at his sides for him to go forwards. King panicked more, spinning and rushing backwards.

While Thomas and King battled, John sat quietly astride me. I tried to ignore King's antics and focus on the tree. I came to realise the flapping fingers were strips of plastic, probably from a haylage bale, one of the ones wrapped in black. It must have blown into the tree during strong winds and been torn and ripped by the branches. It wasn't haunted at all.

I took a tentative step forward to check it out, then another. We slowly made our way towards the gate. I kept my eye on the plastic, just in case I was wrong.

"There we go," John spoke calmly. "Just a bit of black plastic wrap."

I was right. I stopped short of going into the puddle. Closer up it didn't look black, but I still wasn't sure about stepping in it. Behind me I could hear Thomas yelling at King and suddenly I was even more glad of John. He let me stretch my nose down and sniff at the puddle. I snorted at it, watching the water ripple. Slowly, carefully, moving one foot at a time and testing the depth as I went, I made it to the gate. John unlatched it and I splashed through. At its deepest it only came to my fetlock.

"It's ok, it's not deep," I called back to King, looking up proudly as John patted my neck.

Thomas was still booting at King's sides and yelling. Suddenly, with a look of sheer terror on his face, King shot forward, rushed through the gate, jumping, and splashing through the puddle before charging past me.

"Stupid," Thomas cursed.

"Just give him some time," John suggested. "Let him look and see it isn't going to kill him."

"Ha," Thomas barked a laugh. "Like you could get that back through."

I was insulted by being referred to as 'that'. I think John was too, because he picked up the reins and asked me to walk back through the puddle to the other side. I was a little hesitant as I stepped through, but did it, and returned with no hesitation at all, knowing now that the puddle was safe to cross.

Thomas sniffed a bit. "Being soft on horses just spoils them," he huffed, turning King around and heading for the trail.

John shook his head as we were left to close the gate before following them. "If it spoils you," he whispered as he closed the gate, "then how is it that we are the ones that got through with no fuss, and how come we are the ones closing the gate, eh lad?"

He patted me and we turned, jogging to catch up with King. He was tense for the rest of the ride, jumping at every sound and snorting at things I couldn't see. I, on the other hand, loved the rest of the ride, watching the rabbits play and enjoying the scent of the trees.

Chapter 15

It was the evening after our woodland ride. King and I had made it back to the lorry without any major incident, but King had been desperate to get back onto the lorry and leave. I had been happy enough tied up next to Shannon with a hay net while the humans had a picnic, but King had almost tied himself in knots until he was loaded aboard the lorry. Chloe had insisted they leave the ramp down though. She had sat on the end of it, holding Hamish's lead rope and sharing her lunch, or at least some of it, with the dun pony.

Thomas had done little with King when we got back to the lorry. He had just taken off his tack, put it away and tied King up, until he had started messing around outside. John had shaken his head again as King was loaded up and left. He brushed the sweat and dried bits of mud from my body, and even put a little cooler rug over me so as I dried off, I didn't get cold. King got no such treatment. I'm not sure he was even offered a drink until we reached home, while Hamish, Shannon and I were all watered after the picnic when we were cooled.

Back at the yard we had all been given extra feed and apples from Chloe. She didn't dare go into King's stable, but I noticed her slip an apple into his bucket all the same. She had given everyone a little fuss goodnight, but had spent extra time in with Hamish making sure he was happy and comfortable, popping him in a little extra hay since it was a cooler night, before she headed for her own bed.

Alison and John had hung around a little after that and I had realised they were talking about me. John was saying how well I was doing, both in my jumping and my general attitude. I was pleased to hear he thought so highly of me.

"He's a good little jumper; he'll do you proud when he's a bit more confident. Nice jump in him and he is keen to learn."

"That's good to hear, Ryan didn't have much luck with him." Alison sighed.

"Well, he was a boy, and a silly one if you don't mind me saying. A chifney and flash noseband." He shook his head.

"It's a wonder young Lir didn't end up as grumpy as that mare of yours." John laughed, but I glanced at Shannon. It proved to me John did know, he did understand. He had guessed, quite rightly, why Shannon was the way she was. The thought made me happy. John understood. I would be understood.

I tuned back into his and Alison's conversation. He told her all about our encounter with the spooky tree and the puddle. He said I was very brave and had behaved very well indeed. Explaining how he'd been patient with me and I'd done the gate on my own terms with no problems at all. His praise made me feel even prouder about how I had handled my encounter with the tree. John was much less complimentary about Thomas and King. He spoke at length on Thomas's treatment of King, his shouting and kicking, and even how he had treated him after the ride had ended. Once again John had seen everything and understood.

"The horse was terrified," he shook his head. "I'll say one more thing too, I would not let the little one out with them alone on a hack," he glanced   at Hamish. "As good a rider as Chloe is and as honest as that pony..." he shook his head.

Alison also glanced in Hamish's direction. "I know Thomas is a hard rider, but he's a brilliant jumper."

"That may be," John nodded. "But having seen him with that horse spooking and jumping all over the place today," he shook his head. "I'd just make sure she hacks with another rider as well; I think King's a little unpredictable and I reckon Thomas would forget anyone else was there and focus on his battle with the horse."

Alison had nodded. "I see what you mean. Perhaps, if it comes up, you could go along?"

"It would be my pleasure," John smiled.

They had headed out of the stables then, closing the doors against the night. As the dimness settled around us I turned to Shannon, keen to tell her about what had happened to me on the trail with the gate and the tree.

"He was so scared," I said of King. "I've never seen anyone so terrified and all Thomas did was yell at him and boot him in the sides. Even when he tried to run backwards. John just sat and let me work through it, but King got no chance. It was as if as soon as he stopped moving, Thomas started yelling!"

"Well, that's how it is," Shannon sighed, looking over at me sadly. "For competition horses that is."

I looked at her, confused.

"You must have noticed," Shannon said to me. "Competition horses are there to do a job. Most are treated more like a commodity to the humans that have them. There to perform, like machines with no feelings. Their humans will give them everything they need physically while they can compete and win. When they are useful they are cared for, but often they are also disposable if they break, something easily tossed aside and replaced by another who can do what the human wants. That is why King's rider is the way he is. To him King is merely a tool, something he uses to jump, nothing more." She looked over at Hamish.

"You see the difference between Thomas and Chloe. Hamish is Chloe's friend, her pony, her confidant. He is someone she adores and treats as family. He means something to her beyond what he can do for her. I'd go so far as to say he is not only irreplaceable to her, but that she would be heartbroken without him. He's her whole world."

I think I understood, but I didn't like it. "Are all competition horses treated that way?" I asked.

"No," Seamus piped up from the other side of me. "There are humans out there who like to compete and consider their horses partners in it. That will put a horse's welfare first and won't abandon them if they can no longer do the job, but they are few and far between."

"What happens when we can't do the job?" I asked.

I saw Shannon glance at Seamus. "If we are lucky," he said, "we become Hamish." He settled himself as if to doze and I was left to wonder what happens to those who are not so lucky.

"To the humans," Shannon said, "competition is a business. They forget that to us it is our lives." She turned away from me and began to munch on her hay.

It took me a long time to settle that night, and when I did, it was with one thought in my mind. One day, I thought, I want to be like Hamish.

Chapter 16

A few weeks after the hack in the woods, John brought me in from the field, groomed me quickly and fetched my tack. It was unusual. Typically we rode during the morning and never later in the evening, but I quickly realised we were going out with Hamish and King. My mind flicked back to the memory of John saying it would be his pleasure to ride out with Chloe to ensure she wasn't alone with Thomas and King after the tree encounter.

We set off along the lane in the late evening sun. The autumn was clearly well upon us, leaves fluttered down, a myriad of golden-brown hues. King disliked this, swishing his tail at the falling foliage. I liked it. The leaves reminded me that crisp autumn mornings would be here soon and I loved them. Hamish happily stomped along taking in the views and looking for places he could 'suggest' having a trot.

It was the usual route we took, out along the quiet road from the yard, up through a few trees, across a large field and then looping back around to the yard. We knew the circuit well and I absently thought that I could have done the ride on my own with little difficulty. I knew where I was, where home was and how to get there.

Just as we made our way through the top of the trees and out onto the high point furthest from home, I had a strange sensation wash over me. For a second, I felt tense. I knew the others did too, I could see it in their posture, their expressions, and I knew what the feeling meant. Sure enough, a second later we heard it, the low rumble of thunder off in the distance.

Having lived in fields most of my life I have no fear of thunder storms. They come and they pass. If anything, I would stand in the lowest part of my field, bum to the wall for shelter, and once the lightning was done, I would stand under the trees for cover from the rain I knew would follow. King, on the other hand, had no such experience. To him this loud booming sound was to be feared, run away from. He was used to his stable. There, he thought, he was safe.

I watched as King began to try and race forwards. Thomas yelled at him in his usual fashion, digging his heels in and pulling at King's mouth, but this time the large showjumper was having none of it. His ears were flattened, his eyes wide and white. I could have told Thomas what was coming. I expect John could have too, but he was too busy making sure Chloe was safe. John need not have worried; Hamish was as unmoved as I was.

King though plunged forwards, throwing his back feet in the air. Had he given Thomas a second to recover, he may never have unseated his rider, but he didn't. As soon as his back end landed, King flung himself upwards again, twisting sideways as he went. I could see clear air between Thomas and the saddle and I knew without doubt he was hitting the ground.

Thomas landed hard with a thud. King didn't even pause; he ran off down the trail towards home without a second look. I watched Thomas lying on the ground and could think only one thing. It works both ways. If you as a human don't care about us, why should we care about you? King had just proven that point. He'd ditched Thomas and left without a care.

John slid down from me keeping hold of my reins a little more tightly than usual. He didn't need to worry; I wasn't going to follow King. He glanced at me and seemed to realise this, loosening his grip a little. He headed over to Thomas, who sat up a little as another roll of thunder echoed around the hillside, creeping ever closer.

I flicked my ears. We were very exposed on the hill. I didn't like it. Neither, it seemed, did John. He helped Thomas up.

"We need to get away from these trees," he said. Thomas took a step and then nearly fell over again.

"I've done my ankle," he hissed.

John looked over at me, Chloe and Hamish. He shook his head. "Lir can't take us both, we're too heavy," he eyed Chloe. "Em's, do you think Thomas could ride Hamish back, he's a fair stout fella, Thomas wouldn't harm him. You can ride with me on Lir."

I looked from John to Hamish a little worried. Chloe? On me? I suddenly felt a little nervous. Chloe looked scared. She slowly slid from Hamish, her small hands shaking a little. Hamish snorted at Thomas; he looked decidedly unhappy about the whole idea.

"We need to get Chloe home quickly," I pointed out as another rattle of thunder boomed and a flash lit up the sky not so far away.

"Fine," he huffed.

John helped Thomas up onto the little dun. Hamish immediately pinned his ears back, swished his tail and bared his teeth.

"I know," Chloe hugged him. Hamish's ears pointed forwards and he nuzzled her until John called her over. As soon as she left his side, Hamish returned to his scowling. I'm not sure Thomas noticed, but I certainly hoped he did.

John hopped up on me and then helped Chloe clamber up the saddle and perch behind him. She was lighter than I expected. I could feel her tense against my skin. Don't worry Chloe, I thought, I've got you.

We headed home, me walking as if I were carrying glass I was terrified would break, Hamish walking as if he were carrying a sack of potatoes he'd happily dump in a river if he could. The storm was raging and the rain just starting to fall hard when we made it back to the barn. Alison was so relieved when she saw us. She hugged not only Chloe, but also John.

King was already in his stable. He made no sign of being interested in if Thomas was alright or not, and I didn't blame him. John took him away in his car to the human vet, while Meg put us away and dried us off. Chloe was bundled inside to dry as well, but she reappeared later to hug Hamish and give him a carrot. She fetched one for me as well.

"You're both my heroes now," she said, giving us both a hug.

From then on, I became a special favourite of Chloe. She spent more time with me and I got more treats from her in my bucket too. On an evening I was given a hug goodnight as well as a pat. It made me feel very proud. Hamish was pleased with me too, because I had brought her home as safely as he would have. I'll never forget that storm. It taught me a lot about humans and how we view them, and how their treatment of us can hurt them in the worst circumstances.

One thing was certainly true, John had been right about not letting Chloe go alone with Thomas and King. I wondered what would have happened had John and I not been there. The thought made me shudder.

Chapter 17

Chloe was not Alison's only child. She had a son as well, Sean. I'd never seen much of Sean. I knew he rode because sometimes he would take Shannon into the school to jump. The chestnut mare regarded him with apathy, unlike Chloe who seemed to be the only human she adored. I remember asking her why she treated Sean so coldly and she simply replied it was wrong to bite children, but that didn't mean you had to like them. This didn't really answer my question at the time, although it made sense to me later.

Sean really only liked to jump. He never came to the yard to fuss over us as Chloe did, or even to hack out. He even had Meg groom and tack up Shannon for him if he could get away with it. I was surprised therefore when he showed up on the yard one fine morning looking extremely keen. We all soon discovered why. Alison arrived with the lorry shortly afterwards. She lowered the ramp and led a pretty little light grey pony, somewhere in size between Hamish and I, down the ramp. He looked around himself with a look I can only describe as unimpressed and was quickly taken to a stable by Sean.

Over the next few days we came to learn that his name was Dinny. He had been bought from a junior show jumping champion for Sean, and was to be his pony. Dinny had been everywhere and done everything it seemed, at least that is what he said. He'd won ribbons, trophies, he'd even been named champion. He claimed to be very expensive, a fact he seemed rather proud of, although I wasn't sure why.

"My pony is the most expensive on the yard," Sean bragged to Chloe one morning, adding credence to Dinny's own claims.

She didn't reply, just slipped into Hamish's stable, grooming kit in hand, shaking her head. She patted his neck. "But you're worth your weight in gold," she hugged him. "Besides, I bet Sean and Dinny couldn't ride back through a storm like we did." She poked her head over the door and glanced at me.

"Isn't that right Lir," I gave her a little snort of confirmation and she smiled.

"It's not all about what you pay for a pony, or horse," she muttered to us. "It's how well you work together and what you can do for each other." She brushed away some hay from Hamish's mane and kissed his cheek.

Sean soon began to ride Dinny quite a bit. I saw him jumping in the arena and had to admit Dinny was very good at his job. My mind flicked back to Shannon's thoughts on competition horses and I wondered if Dinny realised he was replaceable. He didn't seem to. He'd often come into the barn, head held high, as Sean went on about the competitions he would win.

It never seemed to dawn on Dinny that Sean only ever talked about what he would do, not they. Nor did he appear to notice that the only time Sean spent with him was to ride and jump, never to brush, fuss and hack. That is, at least not at first. It slowly seemed to register with him that the other horses were treated differently and it seemed to surprise him greatly.

He started to watch John with me and Seamus, how he treated us, brushed us and rode. How we went off the yard and came back happy and jogging.

"Where did you go?" he asked one morning. "Is there a competition so close you can ride to it?"

"No," I replied. "We just hacked around the fields and woods."

Dinny looked confused. "What do you mean?"

"Well, we went out," I said not sure how to respond. "Just for fun."

"Yes," Seamus put in. "You know, where you go out for a wander, to see the world. Just, to take a walk."

"I don't think I've ever done that," Dinny replied.

"What!" I exclaimed. "Not even at the place you came from?"

"No," Dinny replied as if thinking hard. "I did pony rallies. They're like big lessons with lots of horses and ponies and trainers. Competitions, oh and a camp once."

"What's camp?" I asked.

"It's where children take their ponies and camp together for a week," Hamish replied around a mouthful of grass. "Chloe's a bit young for it yet, but I did it in my home before here, and I did day visits with her last summer. It's great fun."

"It is," Dinny agreed. "We did a little competition at the end and I won with my first human. She was so pleased she won."

"You mean you won, together, as a team." Hamish pointed out.

Dinny looked confused again. "I suppose."

After that Dinny seemed to watch how Chloe treated Hamish a little more. He watched as she spent hours grooming, bathing and fussing him. How she gave us all treats, but more to myself and Hamish, and how she would sneak us extra hay when it was a cooler night. She would speak to Dinny and include him in her routines, but she was slightly distant from him, I think because he was Sean's.

Dinny began to ask us questions about our lives, about hacking, how we competed and what happened if we did or did not win. We tried our best to answer him honestly, but everything we told him was met with confusion and, inevitably, with him saying that never happened in his life, not that he cared, he was 'just curious'.

As much as he protested his apathy at what we told him, I could tell it wasn't true. He tried to hide that he was jealous of the extra attention that Hamish and I got, but I could tell he was. I came to realise that Dinny was the perfect competition pony and he had never even known it.

He was one of those tools that could be easily replaced, only now he was beginning to see there were other paths in life and it hurt him deeply. He was better off, I thought, not knowing. Better off thinking his life was just how all horses lived. He could have been blissfully boastful, happily haughty, if we hadn't burst his bubble. Now every time Sean came by only to jump him, he knew it was because that was what Sean wanted, not to spend time with him. Equally, he had to watch as Chloe pampered Hamish, lavishing him with love and care.

Even I had John, someone who treated me with respect and kindness. Someone who didn't view brushing my coat as a chore to be done, an unpleasant necessity to allow me to compete without injury. To say I felt sorry for Dinny is an understatement. Every toss of his head, every denial that he cared, only made me feel worse for him.

Shannon found Dinny irritating, despite me telling her what I thought he was going through. She saw him as just boastful and brash. I think she underestimated how differently horses can react to being treated poorly. She had become sour and disliked most humans. Dinny just longed to be loved by one.

Chapter 18

I had done several local competitions with John now. I had learned I disliked travelling, even in the big lorry, but I could cope if we weren't on it for too long. I hated the way it rolled under my feet, always making me feel unsteady, as if I was constantly going to fall over. I'd sweat as I tried to keep my balance. I often found myself remembering Nana's tale of the horses that had come on boats from the far-off land to be shipwrecked on the Irish coast. My ancestors. How must they have felt on those tossed ships, rolling, and rocking so much more than my own lorry. The idea made me shudder. John must have noticed my discomfort when travelling that far because he always arranged for us to go a good half an hour early, so I could cool down and dry off before the class would start.

One of the furthest competitions we went to was in a large sand arena. We mostly competed outside on grass, but as the weather grew damper and cooler, the show jumping moved inside. I may have hated getting there, but I liked the arena. It was bigger than the small patches of green we jumped on outside, and it was always dry. The sand surface was soft and springy too, in fact, the only thing I didn't like were the jumps placed by, or just after the corners. The solid walls of the ring made it feel a little claustrophobic in the corners, and often I felt as if the turns to the fences were somehow tighter there than in our outdoor arena at home.

Not long before Christmas one year, we headed off to the arena for a special Christmas show. There was to be jumping and a fancy dress. I was loaded in the lorry alongside Dinny, Seamus and Hamish. John was to jump Seamus and I, Sean was entered with Dinny into the junior jumping class, and Hamish, dressed as a reindeer, was entering the fancy dress alongside Chloe in a Santa suit.

"The things we do for love," Hamish had sighed as Chloe placed antlers on his head and wove tinsel in his mane so we could see the full effect. I laughed, but mostly because I thought Hamish secretly liked his costume. Dinny, as usual, had been glad he didn't have a Chloe so he didn't have to dress up and look silly.

Since it was cold, Alison had arranged with her friend who ran the arena to put us in stables when we arrived. I had a good view of the ring and watched with interest as others jumped the course of fences that were set out. The adult classes came first. I was in the novice class so my turn came quickly. The course was quite nice, not too scary and nicely spread out. Little Christmas trees had been set up beside some of the jump wings, and the wall, made out of painted wooden 'bricks', had been finished with wreaths on each of its pillars. Overall, I decided it looked quite pleasant. All except one fence, that is. A triple laid out right after the furthest corner. I eyed it a little uncertainly.

John and I did quite well. I cleared all of the fences and in not too bad a time, although I admit I took the jump after the corner very slowly. The fence wasn't as bad as I had expected, but the turn into it was short and demanding. John however, either did not notice my slow approach, or more likely, agreed with me that going steady and clear was better than fast and failing.

I settled myself back into the stable, chatting with Hamish as we watched the classes. Seamus was the next to jump. He was more advanced than I was, jumping much larger fences. Still the course was very similar in layout, they had only added an oxer and raised the poles higher.

Seamus took everything in his stride, popping over the fences as if they were barely there. He was much larger than me and I absently wondered if being larger made it easier, right up until the triple. Seamus made the turn tighter than I had, but I could see him struggle just a little more with it.

When John came out patting Seamus neck, he spotted Sean. "If they leave that triple for the juniors," he remarked. "Take care on the turn, it's really tight."

Sean just shrugged and wandered away towards the little café selling warm drinks. John shook his head. He hopped off Seamus and began brushing him down.

Just after lunch the junior jumping began and the fancy dress. I saw Alison suddenly looking flustered and realised Chloe and Sean's classes were on at the same time. Chloe insisted she and Hamish would be fine alone, but, seeing as she was younger, Alison refused to let her go on her own and walked away with her, leaving Sean and Dinny behind.

John had gone off to get a coffee, while Seamus had dozed off in the corner. Only I seemed to be there to watch the pair enter the ring. The fence layout had changed very little indeed. Most of the poles had been lowered and the triple had become a double, but the tight turn was still there. I willed Dinny to see it and slow down for it.

The first few fences they jumped went well, but then came the double. I knew as soon as I saw Sean haul Dinny tightly into it there was no way he could make the fence. A look of horror crossed Dinny's face as he realised what I already knew. He skidded to a stop clattering into the fence a little, but surprisingly not unseating a pole.

Sean looked furious. He booted Dinny in the sides, whipping him around in a circle to go at the fence again, but something about Dinny looked odd. Sean drove him at the fence growling, but it was no good. Dinny stopped again, the whites of his eyes showing, I saw him drop a shoulder, darting out of the fence and knew that Sean was not coming with him. Sure, enough Sean sailed over the fence landing in the sand.

"Eliminated," the tannoy crackled.

A beetroot red Sean stormed to his feet, snatching Dinny's reins and stomping out of the arena, dragging Dinny with him. I don't think he even cared to stop and think why Dinny refused, or that the first time was his own fault. Dinny hadn't jumped and that was all that mattered to Sean, not why, not if he was hurt or scared. Dinny was a thing that hadn't worked properly.

I glanced over to see Hamish coming back our way. A smiling Santa clad Chloe was sat in the saddle, though she was lying on Hamish's neck, her arms wrapped around him. A 4th place rosette was pinned to his bridle. She looked like the happiest kid in the world. I glanced at Sean huffing and puffing as he yanked the tack off Dinny and stormed away. How could they be so different I wondered?

Chapter 19

When we arrived back at the yard, Sean jumped out of the lorry almost as soon as it stopped. He stormed off towards the house without looking back, his boots slapping across the wet concrete. Alison hopped down from the cab and jogged after him. We had heard most of their conversation on the journey home. Dinny had been silent, listening to Sean go on and on about how bad a pony he was and how useless he was. Sean was uninjured, but his pride had evidently taken a beating and he was going to lay the blame squarely at Dinny's hooves.

Meg came out of the barn as John lowered the ramp. She fetched Dinny, not noticing his flat demeanour, his lowered head, or drooped ears. John took Seamus and Chloe led both me and Hamish. We followed her quietly, still dressed in her tiny red suit, as she guided us under the moonlight. She glanced after her brother and I notice her little face wore a dark, disapproving look. She, I guessed, had not been taken in by Sean's blaming of Dinny.

We were all bundled up into our stables, but the joys of the day had been dampened by Sean and his attitude. Chloe brought us all our feeds, slipping the buckets into our stables one by one, along with treats and hugs, while John unloaded the tack and belongings.

"This is for my special reindeer friend," she giggled as she slipped the bucket inside Hamish's stable. "I dipped the carrot in treacle," she whispered with a snicker. I heard a happy munching sound come from Hamish's box.

"One for the best jumper of the day." She presented Seamus his bucket, complete with apple.

"One for the best novice jumper." I got a hug as well as a carrot and an apple.

"You're the best girl," she patted Shannon.

Then she turned to Dinny. He stood sadly looking at her over his door, his pale grey face shining a little in the moonlight that flooded through the barn door.

"One for the poor pony who has to put up with my brother," she slipped a bucket in with both an apple and a carrot in it. She also stopped for a little while, stroking Dinny's neck and face. "He shouldn't have said those mean things about you." I heard her sniffle a little and realised she was crying. She felt as bad for Dinny as I did.

Closing the door, she said goodnight to us all and headed out of the barn pulling the door closed behind her. Dinny watched her go, a strange look on his face. I realised he'd just received love and kindness for the first time. A little girl had cared about him so much she had shed a tear for him. He looked confused, hurt, glad, lost, perhaps a mixture of them all.

"What was that all about?" Shannon asked from beside me, dragging me away from my thoughts.

"Dinny here ditched Sean over a fence," Seamus almost chuckled. "I wish I'd been awake to see it. Boy could do with dropping a peg or five."

"I didn't do it on purpose," Dinny tried to explain a little indignantly. Chloe's spell on him seemed to break and his old attitude flooded back.

"Shoulder down, bounce out the side of the fence, not on purpose?" Seamus scoffed. "I might have missed seeing it, but it certainly sounds like you meant it, my boy."

"I... it... it... was too tight, we came in to fast and, oh," he took a deep breath. "I couldn't do it."

"It was the double, the one we had as a triple after the corner," I told Seamus. "I saw it."

"It was going alright at first," Dinny cut in, remembering what had happened. "We cleared the first few fences fine and the time was good. He pulled us tight into the wall, but I managed that, just. And I could have done the double, easy, but he pulled me in too tight that time, even tighter than the wall. I couldn't have cleared the fence, there was no way. I stopped, just, but I slid as I did, I hit my leg off the jump wing, right off the chunky upright bit as he hauled me around, I just caught it. It hurt so much, and it went, I don't know, almost numb.

I've hit my legs off a pole before, but nothing like this. When he pulled me around to go again, I wasn't ready. My leg felt funny, painful but also like it wasn't there. I tried to go, but it felt so odd. I wasn't sure if I was getting my paces or strides right, I couldn't work it all out. I think I panicked. I'd jumped out the side before. Saoirse always stayed on. I thought he would too."

"Dead leg," Seamus nodded. "Happened to me once out on a cross country course, hung a leg a little low over a hedge and clipped a rail I didn't see. Hurt's like nothing else, a weird, tingly feeling, wears off after a little bit."

"Yes, but it's scary if it's never happened to you before," Dinny pointed out. Seamus had to agree with that.

Shannon shook her head. "You should have just tried to make the jump anyway."

I looked at her surprised. "But he was hurt," I protested. "I mean, I know it wasn't badly, but he didn't know that at the time, it could have been serious."

"Mark my words," Shannon sighed. "Worse will come of this than jumping with a sore leg. He dumped Sean, that will come back to haunt him, even if Sean was in the wrong. You think it will be the boy that pays for this? No, it'll be Dinny. That's how it works. Dinny threw the boy, Dinny will pay."

"That's not fair," I pointed out. "Sean caused the problem, not Dinny. He shouldn't have turned so tightly into the fence, and after he should have trotted around a little, made sure he was sound before trying to jump again. John always does that with me, even if I only clip a pole."

"Fair!" Shannon let out a snort. "What about our lives seem fair to you Lir? We do what we need to in order to survive in the human's world. Face it, life is not fair. What Dinny did will be punished. That's the way the humans are. We are the ones who pay the price, whether it was our fault or theirs."

"Not all humans," Hamish pointed out. He lifted his head to peer over the door, his nose had a smear of treacle on it and he licked at it as he spoke. "If that were true Chloe wouldn't have said what she did to Dinny. It's clear she thinks her brother was wrong."

"Indeed," Shannon sighed. "But unfortunately for us Chloe is a slip of a girl and as likely to have her voice heard as we are."

I looked from Shannon to Dinny and back. Was she right? Would Dinny suffer because of Sean's mistake? I couldn't believe it, but my mind flicked back to Sean storming away across the yard. He was Dinny's human, like it or not, and he certainly didn't seem to understand, or care to try and understand his pony. I suddenly felt sorry for Dinny all over again.

Chapter 20

In the end Shannon would have been proven right if it hadn't been for John. Alison stormed onto the yard first thing the next morning ready to 'deal with' Dinny. She seemed almost as mad at him as Sean had been the evening before. I watched as she blazed into the barn, her anger clear and her eyes fixed on the little white-grey pony. I felt my heart clench a little, wondering what she had planned for him. Judging by the lunge whip and lines she carried it wasn't anything fun, but John followed her into the barn carrying my saddle and bridle.

"Morning Alison," he smiled and she paused. "Are you taking Shannon out? I was going to take young Lir for a little hack myself. I don't think it's fair to make him work hard after yesterday." He put my saddle down and gave my neck a pat and then seemed to notice the lunging equipment in her hands.

"Actually, I was intending to show Sean's pony a thing or two," she replied eyeing Dinny. "Get him lunging over a few fences."

"Ah, well, to be honest with you, if you want to sort out the reason he didn't jump that double yesterday, it's not the pony you want to show a thing or two, it's Sean." He lifted my saddle over the door as he spoke, giving me a smile. I think my ears pricked up at him. Was John really going to defend one of us?

"Excuse me?" Alison asked a little indignantly.

John turned around to face her and I poked my head out over the door next to his shoulder so I could see her.

"I was coming back with my coffee when he went into the ring; I saw his round. There was no way that pony could have made the jump the first time, Sean pulled him into the fence far too tightly. I warned him about that when I jumped it as a triple. The corner was sharp. To be fair it's a good job the pony stopped, if he'd tried to make the fence, Sean could have had a far worse accident." John shook his head.

"No, I'm afraid first refusal is on Sean, and the second, I reckon." He walked over to Dinny's stable and pulled the door open, he felt down his foreleg. "Yep, feel for yourself, there's heat just here," John left his hand lingering a little on a spot just above Dinny's fetlock.

"I bet he clipped the fence, maybe the jump wing, trying to stop. Sean should have walked or trotted him round in a big circle first, made sure he felt sound before trying again, rather than rushing back to the jump straight away. You can't ask a sore horse to jump. Imagine banging your elbow off something hard, getting that numb feeling and then being asked to lift a weight."

Alison was bending down now feeling Dinny's leg. The anger on her face had melted away to a look of something else, shame perhaps I wondered, or maybe embarrassment. She took him out of the stable in a headcollar and walked him up and down a few times watching him move. John then took his rope and trotted him for Alison to watch him. There was, I noticed, a very small bob of his head on one stride. Dinny was slightly lame. Alison began to look more and more annoyed, but this time I was pretty sure Dinny was not the reason why, nor did I think he would be the recipient of her wrath.

John led Dinny back to his stable and put him inside, bolting the door closed and tossing some hay in for him. At that moment Chloe skipped into the barn, her usual cheery self. Spotting my tack on the door her grin grew wider.

"Hi John! Are you riding out, can I come, please, mum, can I go?" John smiled and Alison just nodded, still glancing at Dinny.

"I dare say Dinny will be fine, a bit of cold hosing and a couple of days rest, he'll be fit as a fiddle," John smiled kindly. "Do you want me to ask Meg to hose him down?"

"No," Alison shook her head. "I think Sean should." She turned and left the barn.

"Sean won't," Chloe piped up heading over to Dinny and giving him a pat. "He's lazy."

John laughed. "Come on, let's get you tacked up."

Our ride wasn't a long one, and when we came back, I saw that Meg was indeed hosing Dinny's leg. He stood quietly letting her run the cool water over his sore spot without protest. As we came back, I saw Alison come out of the house and walk over to us.

"Nice ride?" she asked.

Chloe nodded. "We cantered up Hamish's hill."

"And Hamish won," John added with a knowing smile.

"John, would you mind taking Hamish to the barn with Lir?" Alison asked. "I'd like to ask Chloe something."

"Sure," John took Hamish's reins and led us away. As we walked though, we could hear Alison ask Chloe if she would like to take on Dinny to jump and show. I saw her shake her head a little.

"I like him," she said in her small sweet voice. "But I have Hamish and he's perfect. Besides, Dinny's a bit too big."

He was. Chloe would have been a pea sat on a drum on Dinny. I felt sorry for him all over again. Hamish and I agreed not to tell him Chloe had turned down the opportunity to take him on. It would have broken his heart, especially since I was certain that big or not, Dinny would have treated Chloe as if she were the most precious thing in the whole world. Because she was the very first person who had ever cared about him rather than his jump.

For several months after that day, Dinny's life was one of leisure. He was turned out with us, occasionally lunged by Alison and groomed by Chloe. He slowly began to become a different horse. Affection and love stripped him of his haughtiness. Not jumping proved to him there was more to life than classes and shows, though I know he missed being ridden and often longed to go out with Chloe. Hamish and I would simply exchange glances when he'd mention how much he hoped she'd come and hack him out.

The winter took firm hold and Dinny grew a thick fluffy coat that he'd never really known he had, as most winters he had been clipped out fully and rugged. Even I had to admit he looked very sweet with his winter coat left on. I think he would have been happy enough to have life stay just as it was, but one morning, as spring rolled around, Alison brought the lorry to the yard. Dinny was loaded aboard and driven away. We knew he'd been sold and I hoped to somewhere nice. I tried to imagine he had gone to a bigger version of Chloe, to someone who loved him, groomed him and hacked him around. The thought of him going back to his old life as a show jumping pony made me feel too sad.

Chapter 21

My life over the next spring, summer and autumn was a whirlwind of shows and competitions with John. I didn't mind it most of the time, especially when the places were local and I could go with Hamish, Shannon or Seamus. Some outings it was only King and I. These were less fun, often larger, further away affairs. Thomas was never interested in smaller shows.

I loathed the lorry on longer journeys. Every time I went on it, I felt hemmed in. I hated the movement of the floor and the shudder of the engine's vibrations traveling through my hooves to the top of my ears. Shannon would always sympathise with me, but she would always end by telling me to keep the humans happy. So long as they were happy, I would be alright.

By the middle of summer, I found myself in the same classes as Seamus. We didn't care which of us came first, but Alison did. She began to take a little more notice of me now I was bringing home ribbons like Seamus did, and sometimes even placing higher than the large coloured horse.

I finally felt I had settled into my new life. John was kind and a good rider. I had friends, places to go out, and just enough free time of my own to not feel overwhelmed. Sure, there were days when I'd be bundled off into the horrible lorry for an hour's drive to a huge, busy competition and I'd envy Hamish, left behind in the field knowing full well later on Chloe would come and brush him, but those days weren't my entire life.

John and I began to be noticed at a few of the competitions. He told me once as he was tacking up, that I was getting a lot of compliments on my jump. He said it as if it was a good thing, but my mind couldn't help but flick back to Dinny. That was what people had said about him too and he had become nothing more than a jumper with no feelings. John wasn't like that, but at the back of my mind I also knew he didn't own me, Alison did. It's a business Shannon had said. I was a commodity and I was worth more than when we had started.

I voiced these fears to Shannon and Seamus, but both told me not to worry, being worth more was a good thing. Having value to a human didn't mean I'd be sold on for profit, in fact the opposite was more likely – it would make them more likely to keep me.

As the summer turned into autumn the shows slowed down. Once again, we began to compete more indoors than outdoors. We'd travel to the big arena, and I often looked out to see if I could spot Dinny. I didn't. It made me both happy and sad. I wanted to know he was alright, but I could also keep my dream of him hacking around the countryside alive when I didn't spy him.

I remember one autumn show at the arena better than most. Surprisingly it wasn't one of the biggest competitions I went too, nor was it the highest place I got. There is a darker reason I remember it so well.

Just like they had at Christmas, the arena held a Halloween theme show. The jumps were decorated with smiling pumpkins, the poles painted orange, purple and black. This time there were kids' games as well as fancy dress. My going was a last-minute decision. Chloe was desperate to go with Hamish, but Alison was reluctant. She wanted Seamus fit for a bigger event a week later and she didn't want to take Hamish alone. That was when John suggested I try my first intermediate class indoors. He said it would be a good practice. Alison agreed and so off we went.

Just as we had done at Christmas we had stables near the main arena. I watched the other horses jumping closely, more so now than ever before. I felt a little nervous about the class and watching their strides helped me stay calm. I'd jumped that big before, but only outdoors. The tight corners weighed on my mind much more than the spooky jumps that had been created.

I think John could tell I was anxious. He let me take my time going into the ring and we trotted around a few times before signalling we were ready. The course started with a large oxer of purple poles with fillers beneath painted with crescent moons. Once my feet landed clear over that first fence my nerves cleared and I knew I could do the rest.

We came 4th overall, which pleased John enormously. Even Alison was impressed. Hamish won the fancy dress with Chloe dressed up as a ghost rider and pony. They also got a few rosettes from the games.

Chloe had started a tradition at the start of spring. The smaller prizes we won at local shows were displayed on the top doors of our stables. Hamish's door was covered with ribbons, pictures of them together and, at this present time, a picture of a pumpkin Chloe had drawn. We ate our suppers as she fastened her new red rosette in place on the door and then came to my stable with her little plastic stool and pinned my 4th in place. She smiled at me over the door before skipping out of the barn.

Halloween was a few days after. It was a big celebration, bonfires were lit, and this year, unfortunately, the man who had bought the farm across from us, had built his bonfire close by. I had seen it grow larger and larger over the past few weeks on my rides through the countryside. It didn't scare me then, but it would later.

Halloween evening was cool and clear. Chloe rode Hamish in the dusk dressed up in a witch's costume. She gave us all treats before she closed the barn that night, even King got an apple in his bucket. The dark of night spread over the barn and we settled down. I could hear people far off in the field the bonfire was in, just laughter and sounds of joy in the distance.

Then came the first bang and the barn lit up in an array of colours. I didn't know what a firework was, and might have panicked if it wasn't for Shannon.

"Ignore it, it's fine," she mumbled. "It's just a firework."

"It sounds a little close though," Seamus muttered.

They did sound close, but I soon grew used to the sound. That was until one bang that was much louder. It was as if the rocket had gone off right by the back of the barn, close to where the hay was stored. Then everything went silent. The banging stopped.

"The last one's always loudest," Shannon huffed.

A few minutes later though the distinct smell of smoke wove its way through the barn, to my nostrils. I think I was the first to realise what had actually happened. One of the human's fireworks had gone astray, hit the barn roof and tumbled into the wood and hay. Our home was on fire and I wasn't sure anyone even knew.

Chapter 22

Shannon began to batter at the door as soon as she realised that the barn was on fire, first pushing at it with her chest and then kicking at it with both back feet. We could see the flickering light coming from the direction of the hay pile now, and I was sure the barn was growing warmer. I wondered in terror if anyone would notice since the side of the barn on fire was the furthest from Alison's house.

Hamish began to call loudly, hoping to attract attention, while Seamus eyed up the door wondering if he could jump out, but I knew I couldn't fit through the gap, so the large coloured horse wouldn't stand a chance. King, whose stable was closest to the hay simply spun around and around, all his senses leaving him completely.

I began to panic. My heart raced as I watched those flames dance and climb higher and higher up the back wall of the barn. I was trapped. We all were. I wondered if we'd burn or be killed by the barn collapsing around our ears.

There were shouts now, human shouts. Evidently the bonfire party had realised the barn was on fire and had rushed to tell Alison. I looked about frantically realising in horror it was too late. Outside was black night. John, Meg, Thomas, none of them were here. I knew for a fact Alison and Chloe were the only people on the yard. Alison's husband and Sean were away at the cinema. Chloe had told us as much that morning. The only one who could free us was Alison, on her own.

Slowly and steadily the flames began to reach the edges of our stables. I could feel the heat from them. Thick, black smoke began to fill the barn. Shannon somehow managed to kick her door free, the bolt popping off and clattering onto the concrete floor. She shot through the door and skidded to a stop in the open area of the barn, she glanced at me with fear in her dark eyes.

"Go!" I shouted. "Get out, run."

She looked at me a moment longer and ran for the doors, her chestnut coat glinting in the flickering light of the flames. Chloe had not quite closed the large barn doors fully. Shannon pushed her head and neck through the gap, wiggling to open them just enough to escape into the night.

A gust of fresh air flooded in for a second, fanning the flames and pushing them higher. I coughed and called out. Then I heard Chloe's voice from the doorway.

"I have to get him, mum, no, please."

A second later Alison appeared through the smoke. She unbolted Hamish's door and dragged him out towards the barn door. A second later I heard Chloe crying and Alison was back, wrapping a scarf around her face and hauling a terrified looking Seamus out of his stable.

"Lir, mum, Lir!" Chloe's pleading voice screeched. It was mingled with a new sound, a high-pitched wail that seemed to be getting closer with every second. The heat of the fire was so intense I wanted to close my eyes.

Then Alison was at my door, coughing. I could barely see through the smoke, and I'm sure she was struggling too. She threw a rope over my neck. She looked at me with a pleading look and I knew what she wanted. She wanted me to be calm and steady.

It took everything I had not to run, not to push past her and bolt. I stepped out of my stable and glanced at the wild beast that was King, throwing himself at the door. I think I knew right then that

Alison wouldn't be able to save him alone. He'd probably have killed her, or badly injured her if she'd gotten close.

The ribbons on my door began to curl from the heat. I watched as if in slow motion as the green shiny prize I had claimed so recently began to smoulder. Alison put pressure on the rope and I followed her through the haze of smoke out into the night.

I was put into the field with Shannon, Hamish and Seamus. Chloe was there too, clinging to Hamish as if he might disappear. A few people, from the bonfire party, I assumed, had come to help, but did little more than look on.

The wailing sound intensified and a large red lorry appeared, blue flashing lights on the top strobed the barn with a cool light. I could hear King barging about and screaming. Alison went straight to the men who were pulling lengths of hose out.

"I have one horse in there still," she said breathlessly. "I can't get him out."

"We'll try and save it," one man replied turning the hoses on and sending a jet of water onto the barn. "Where's the stable?"

"At the back of the barn," Alison pointed.

"Train the hoses there," the firefighter ordered. He and another man followed Alison to the barn doors. She pointed inside. The men went in and for a while I thought perhaps King might be saved after all.

We stood for a long time by the fence, huddled together for comfort. We wrapped Chloe in the middle, shielding her from the sight of the barn as the flames engulfed it and from the sight of the firefighters emerging and shaking their heads. I glanced at Shannon who lowered her own. We couldn't shield Chloe from the sound of King calling frantically. That sound still haunts me to this day, as I imagine it does everyone there that night. What was almost worse though was the silence that came when his shouts stopped.

The barn burnt on for over three hours with the men desperately trying to put it out. John and Meg arrived, along with Thomas. It was the first time I ever saw Thomas show feeling for King. I felt angry that the showjumper had to die for Thomas to show any emotion about him. Alison, with her black, tear stained face pulled Chloe into her arms and cried alongside her, before John ushered them both back to the house.

He and Meg had inspected us for any immediate injury. Shannon had scrapes along her back and sides, and I kept coughing thanks to the thick smoke. It felt as though my lungs couldn't take in enough air, even outside in the paddock.

I heard John call the vet. "No," he said. "Everyone who can be saved is out." He glanced at Thomas. "First thing will be fine, not much you can do in this light anyway. No, no burns, but they need a good check over. I'll clean Shannon's cuts up and spray them over, just so they're clean. Great, thanks, we'll see you then."

Finally, as the pink hues of dawn cast themselves over the field, the fire was totally dowsed. The back of the barn was merely a tangle of blackened ash and half burnt timbers. The roof was gone and I could see that only one wall of my stable remained. The pictures, rosettes and drawings on Hamish's door were tarnished with soot, blackened around the edges, the ribbons curled and charred.

Chapter 23

We spent hours huddled together in the paddock silently watching as the sun rose higher in the sky. I know we all felt the loss of King, but none of us seemed to know what to say about it. I know I was still trying to block his shouts from my mind as the first rays of warm sun hit my back making me shudder just a little. In the better light we could see more clearly. My grey coat was streaked with soot and ash, as was Seamus's, though it was less visible on his darker patches. Hamish seemed unscathed, but Shannon had deep scrapes on both her sides, the hair missing completely. I coughed again, my chest feeling like it was heavy and full. My lungs had felt as if they were burning in the heat of the barn, now they just felt tight and sore.

The barn was destroyed. We'd known it was bad the night before, but once the sun was fully up, it became clear we wouldn't be using it again. John said as much when he appeared. He and Meg checked on us first thing and then picked through part of the barn, seeing what could be salvaged from the ashes. I watched as they pulled out brushes, rugs and headcollars. One I realised was Kings. I glanced at the others and knew instantly they felt the same as I did.

"If," Shannon began, so quietly I almost didn't hear her. "If only he'd trusted the humans."

It was surprising to hear from her. Of all of us she was the least trusting. I glanced at her as did Hamish.

"I know that sounds odd coming from me," Shannon huffed. "But even I would trust the humans in an emergency."

"He couldn't," Seamus nodded sadly.

Hamish nodded. "Aye, he couldn't even be nice to Chloe. What chance did anyone have with him if he couldn't trust her?"

We shuffled a little closer together, somehow feeling the need to feel each other's presence. Chloe almost ran to the field as soon as she was awake. She scrambled over the gate and rushed to us, pulling Hamish into a hug, her small pale face streaked with tears that spilled again as soon as she was holding him.

I watched as she wrapped her fingers in his mane and clung to him as if he would turn to dust. After a few moments sobbing into his neck, she pulled back a little looking at the rest of us. She slowly disentangled herself from Hamish and walked over to Shannon, her eyes traced the scrapes on her side. She gently rubbed Shannon's nose, giving it a little hug. Seamus was next. Chloe couldn't really reach his head, so she hugged his leg instead. He lowered his muzzle and snuffled at her head.

Finally, she turned to me, more tears flowing as she walked over and wrapped her small arms around my neck. Her body felt warm against me and I snuggled into her a little. She dusted some of the ash from my coat. We ended up stood around her, a little huddle of equines and a small human sharing our sorrow and pain.

Eventually John came into the field. He eased Chloe away, though it was clear she didn't want to leave us for a second.

"It's alright sweetie," he smiled, but he looked sad. "They'll be alright for a bit, go get yourself some breakfast."

Chloe looked back over her shoulder at us as he ushered her back towards the house. I saw Alison by the gate. She looked dishevelled and almost as upset as we were.

Arthur, one of the vets from our practise turned up a little while later. He was a jolly, older man, but even his face fell when he saw the barn. He checked us over one by one, examining us for burns or cuts, checking our heart rate and listening to our breathing with his little stethoscope. It was cold on my hair.

Finally, he had us trot up and checked us again. I struggled with the trot up. It felt as though I couldn't get enough air in to breath properly. It was hard just doing a few steps and I found myself tired and coughing after just trying. At 10 years of age, my body was badly damaged. Arthur looked at me with a worried look on his face. He listened to my heart and chest again.

Alison was on the yard now. I watched as Arthur turned to her with a serious look on his face.

"What's the verdict?" she asked.

"Well, Seamus will be fine in a day or so, and Hamish seems to be in good health," he glanced at Shannon. "The mare's scrapes are deep. She's going to be off a while until they heal up, but I don't think it'll be too long, it's more where they are than anything."

"And Lir?"

Arthur's face fell a little, he rubbed his chin. "Smoke's gotten in his lungs, there's some damage there. He might get back to jumping, but I wouldn't like to guarantee it. He'll certainly need at least a year out for them to heal up. We'll just have to see how he goes."

Alison looked over at me. "Could he be sold as is?"

My ears pricked. Sold. She would sell me? After all of this? I glanced at Shannon. She had been right all along. I was a commodity to the humans, worthless if I couldn't do my job. I felt like my heart would break.

"NO!"

I looked up and spotted Chloe stood indignantly her hands on her hips. Her lower lip wobbled a little. "We aren't selling Lir," she said her voice wavering a little.

Alison bent down level to her. "Chloe, we can't have horses that can't earn their keep."

"Well, he could be mine, for when I get big," she gulped looking from her mother to me and back.

"Aw, sweetie," she smiled down at Chloe. "It'll be a long time before you are big enough for Lir."

"But we can't sell him," Chloe sobbed. I looked at her feeling torn, clearly at least one human loved me for more than my jumping ability. Alison glanced at me and back at the sobbing Chloe.

"Ok," she looked up at Arthur. "We could loan him out." I think everyone, including me stopped and looked at her.

"We could find someone to take Lir for his rehab, see how he comes on. Maybe if he comes back to full health he could come back. If not we can find him a good home."

Chloe didn't look happy about this, but we all knew from looking at Alison it was the best solution we were going to get. That was it. I was moving on again. Chloe walked over to me and held onto my leg for a while before her mother took her away leaving me alone with my friends. Once more we gathered in a huddle, once more feeling like we were lost with no words to say. I glanced at the barn, hating for a second those humans who had put their fireworks, their party, ahead of our safety. If it wasn't for them King would still be alive and I wouldn't be being sent away to who knows where.

Chapter 24

I stayed at Alison's yard for a few weeks after the fire. It seemed strangely tense, the threat of me leaving hanging over us all. A few people came to see me. Most were put off by my coughing and the damage I had from the fire. A couple of others didn't seem to mind, but Chloe vetoed them. I thought perhaps she was trying to keep me as long as she could.

Men came and took the remains of the barn down, while others came and put up a new one next to the little isolation box. One morning a young girl came to see me. She was older than Chloe, but with a gentle manner and a friendly smile. She spent a lot of time chatting to Chloe and saying how cute Hamish was. I think that helped her case with Chloe.

I found from listening to her chat with Chloe, that the girls name was Emma. She lived in Kilkenny and wanted to be a riding instructor and to work with horses but couldn't afford to buy her own. Emma was desperate to learn everything about horses and horsemanship, and she was hoping I could help her.

She didn't care about my damaged lungs, or the fact I would need rehabilitation, although she looked relived to find out Alison had insurance for me that would cover most of the costs.

So, there it was. Chloe had finally found someone good enough for me. I was to go to Kilkenny with Emma. Alison agreed to take me to the little yard she had found a place at.

So, one cold morning I said goodbye to Shannon, Hamish and Seamus, and walked up the ramp of the horsebox to go to my new home. John was there to see me off. I couldn't be sure, but I think his eyes looked a little misty as I stepped onto the ramp. Chloe brought Hamish out onto the yard. They stood together and waved me goodbye as the box engine sprang to life and we trundled away.

I found myself wondering if I would ever see any of my friends again. I wished them all the best with all my heart, hoped they would stay safely together, or if not, that they would go on to good homes with good humans.

I stepped off the lorry not sure what to expect, but I was pleasantly surprised. Emma's yard was little more than a string of fields and a small cube of stables opposite a barn that held hay and shavings. I was a little relieved that the barn was nowhere near the stables, but it seemed we didn't use them much anyway.

Emma put me in a little paddock and within seconds I heard the thunder of hooves and three horses appeared in the field on the other side of the fence. They looked at each other and then at me.

"Hi! I'm Daisy," a small dark chestnut pony with a thick, tufty blonde mane said sticking her nose over the fence. "This is Oscar," she glanced at a tall Irish Draught to one side of her. "And Wizzy, well his name is Wizard really, but we call him Wizzy. It's ironic really, he's not really that much of a runner."

The black gelding beside her looked a little offended at her comment. "I'm an Andalusian Arab," he said with a toss of his long black mane.

Daisy glanced at him. "But you don't run around the field like I do!"

The gelding sighed. "I have better things to do."

"Like eat," Oscar muttered. Daisy chuckled and Wizzy pulled a grumpy face at her.

"What's your name?" Wizzy asked.

"Lir," I replied.

"Well, welcome Lir, who's your human?" Daisy asked.

"Em," I glanced around a little. It was sort of complicated. Alison still owned me I guessed, but I suppose Emma was the one looking after me. "Emma."

"Oh, she's nice," Daisy said dancing on the spot a little. "She's helped out here before. I like her. She's too big to ride me of course. I have a couple of children that ride me."

Over the next few days, I chatted over the fence with my new friends and learnt a lot about them. I missed Seamus, Shannon, and Hamish, but my new field mates, as they soon became, were friendly and welcoming. Daisy was chatty and always cheerful, followed around by Oscar. I found myself often with Wizzy. He liked to eat quietly, and with my injured lungs, that suited me very well.

I settled in at my own pace, happy not to be rushing to competitions. Life became slow and peaceful. Emma turned out to be much more like Chloe than I had expected. She groomed me daily, spent time with me and even had several people come to check me over, in addition to the vet. The farrier was more than happy with my feet, but the equine dentist found ulcers and bruises in my mouth. I had almost forgotten they were there. John had been so much lighter on the reins than Ryan and I had become numb to the last remaining sore spots. Emma however was mortified to find I had any issues at all and spent a long time asking the dentist about how I had gotten them and how to prevent them in the future. Like my lungs, it seemed, the sore spots would improve in time.

The next human Emma had out to meet me was a small, friendly, blonde woman called Fiona. Wizzy said she was an equine physio. She moved my legs in different ways, had me bend down between my front legs to bite a carrot, and then proceeded to rub various parts of me. She identified every bit of me that was sore and when she had finished, I felt much better. If it hadn't been for my damaged lungs I might have run around the field with joy.

"Well, soreness-wise he'll be fine in a few months," Fiona said as Emma let me off into the paddock. "I'll come back in 3 months and check how he's doing.

The lungs," she sighed. "Well, I think he'll get over that," she patted my neck. "He's got a good attitude. You'll be ok, won't you," she smiled at me as she rubbed my head and I nuzzled at her pocket hoping she might have another carrot. She giggled and dug one out for me.

"I hope so," Emma said with a smile patting my neck. "But even if we can't do anything too athletic, there are tons of things we can do so long as the vet says it's ok. Some groundwork and in-hand work maybe."

My ears perked up at those words. In-hand work. Lucy had done in-hand work. Did this mean Emma knew the things Lucy did? My heart leapt a little. Emma was turning out to be one of those rare humans. One who cared and knew what they were doing. I might, I thought, just have landed on my feet. I wandered off into the field to find Wizzy, thinking that Chloe might just have helped me find a good place to be. I missed her then, but I was incredibly grateful for her.

Chapter 25

Over the next six months Emma spent hours with me. She gave me the most attention I think I had ever had in my life. She would come to the stables and groom me, sometimes putting me in one of the stables for a while so I could nap and be brushed in the dry. She'd even sit on a little stool in the corner doing her homework and asking me what I thought of her answers to the questions she had. I'd snort a response every now and again, she'd smile and say things like 'You're right Lir, it doesn't sound right' or 'I agree, that is a good response, isn't it.'

In the school we started doing liberty work. At first it was only for short periods and in walk, so I didn't get out of breath. But I was finding as the days ticked by that my lungs felt less tight and I could catch enough oxygen in them to not feel so tired when I moved around.

It took me a while to understand what Emma wanted from me, but she was patient and I began to slowly comprehend what she was asking me to do. She especially seemed to like it when I followed her, or came to her when she arrived at the field. I'd get scratches and sometimes a treat when I did well.

I'm not sure when I realised I loved Emma, but I did. She became my whole world. She was the Chloe to my Hamish. I'd finally found my human, one who was all mine. That may sound selfish, but it's true. I didn't mind Emma patting and talking to Wizz, or looking after Daisy when her family went on holiday for a week, because I knew she was mine and I was hers.

Eventually we began to do some in-hand groundwork. It was familiar, thanks to Lucy, but Emma did things a little differently. Plus it had been a long time since I had done such work, so it took a while for me to remember what I was being asked. But I picked things up quickly.

I remember one of our in-hand sessions better than the others. It was a bright morning and Emma set up a series of complicated looking patterns out of poles in the school. We walked over them in different ways, me following her, stepping sideways, backing up and yielding one way and another. Our sessions had grown in length to around 20 minutes, but they were still all in walk. We'd always end with some liberty work. This morning was no different, only Emma decided she would clear the poles away while I was in the school. I remember her saying it was because Daisy's human, a little girl called Annie, was supposed to have a lesson shortly.

I pleased myself wandering around the school. One side of it was fringed with trees that blocked out the wind and in the sun, provided cool shade. I wandered over to them, and considered trimming some of the lower branches as a snack. I had just fixed my sight on a particularly green looking leaf when a loose twig fell from the tree behind me and landed squarely on my rump. All horses are prey animals, and as brave as I consider myself, I am no different. The moment that twig landed on me I shot across the school as if my life depended upon it, only stopping to realise what had happened when I felt safe. I stood as tall as I could and snorted loudly in the direction of the trees. Then I saw Emma laughing and realised what had happened.

"Silly, it was only a twig," she giggled. Then she stopped, her mouth making a little O shape. Her eyes went wide.

"You cantered," she almost whispered. "You cantered and you're not out of breath."

I realised she was right. I hadn't done more than a couple of strides of trot since I'd arrived, always fearful that I could no longer do it given my lungs. But in that moment I realised I could, I hadn't - not because I couldn't, but because I was worried I couldn't. I walked over to Emma putting my nose in her hand. She wrapped her arms around me, pulling me into a hug and I realised she was crying, not out of sorrow, not out of pain, but out of happiness. Happiness for me because I had done something we weren't sure I'd ever do again.

A few days later the vet came out to see me. He listened to me breathe, watched me walk and trot a little and then listened again.

"There's definite improvement," he said with a big smile. "A definite improvement. I think we can gently add more work in. The fitter he becomes the better his lung capacity will be. You can probably up the in-hand work in the school a little more, maybe up to half an hour and add in a little bit of trot here and there, and increase that steadily. Oh, and walks, walks are good, not too long but maybe with some hill work if you can."

"We can," Emma smiled. She pointed to the trackway I'd seen Wizzy go off down regularly on his shorter hacks.

"Grand," the vet smiled and patted me. I looked down the trail eagerly. I missed hacking and walks. I realised my world had become small, and while I liked it in one way, the idea of going exploring with Emma was very appealing.

Since I'd never been out with Emma before, we were accompanied by Wizzy on our first walk. I walked shoulder to shoulder with Emma, while following Wizzy's black rump down the track flicking my ears about and taking in every sight, smell, and sound. It was wonderful to be out seeing things again and my heart soared. From then on, once a week, we went out on a walk together. It was always my favourite day.

Wizzy was not worried by most things. It surprised me as much as it does many humans that an Andalusian crossed with an Arab could be so cool headed and calm, but I came to realise that, like me, he was like that because he'd seen so many things.

A bird would fly out of the hedge and he'd simply mutter something about stupid birds and carry on. I found I liked walking out with him, we would both stop and wait if we did spy something scary, though in fact it didn't happen often. I was pleased that both Emma and Wizzy's 'mum' as she referred to herself, would simply wait until we were comfortable to go past. Wizzy's mum would often pat him as he went by whatever we had spied, but she'd call him a wuss at the same time, giggling as we went.

Chapter 26

Emma liked to read a lot, especially about horses. She'd often sit perched on a little stool and read articles from her horse magazine aloud to me while I ate my dinner. I learnt a lot from those magazines. It seemed like a lot of humans understood us well, and were determined to teach others what they knew. I liked that. I liked more that Emma wanted to learn. She, I decided, would never do anything to deliberately harm me and was trying her best to be the best human a horse could want. I think that made me love her even more.

One dark evening as I buried my nose in a bucket of nuts and carrots, Emma began reading an article about bits and bitless riding. I'd always assumed there was a reason we wore bits. Everyone I had met had been ridden in one. I of course knew that some were more comfortable than others, and how a human's heavy hands could make them painful, even bruise our mouths, but the idea we didn't need them at all was new.

Emma read aloud about how the right bit meant the difference between a happy healthy horse, and one with a sore, painful mouth. She glanced up at me with a little frown on her face.

"That's what happened to you," she said. "The bit caused the bruises and ulcers the dentist found when you first came."

If I could have told her she was right I would have. She looked back at the magazine carrying on reading the article aloud. I listened carefully as she read part of the article written by a top vet. He said that many horses he'd examined after they had passed away had moderate to significant mouth damage. I thought about that for a second. I wondered if I already had such damage, or if I didn't, if I would by the time I was old.

I wondered what a bitless bridle would feel like. Would it make me feel freer? Like I was being ridden in a headcollar? Emma mentioned different types, ones that crossed over under our chins, others that worked with side pulling action. I wasn't sure I liked the sound of the ones that tightened around our noses, thinking back to the flash and how it felt not be able to breathe properly.

I stood half listening to Emma, half wondering what a bitless bridle would be like to use. I decided it would be at least something to experience. It certainly sounded gentler than the bit.

"A bitless bridle could be interesting to try," Emma concluded looking up at me with a smile. "I mean, I don't think my hands are heavy, but even still."

I snorted at her in agreement. We'd never ridden together before, but she had a habit of never pulling on the lead rope as we walked shoulder by shoulder – something that I loved and I thought boded well for her riding style. She looked at me, her head tilted just a little to one side as if she were contemplating something.

I forgot all about the bitless bridle article after that night - that is until the equine dentist paid me another visit.

His name was Conor. He was a tall, broad man with a jolly face and a kindly manner. He brought with him an assortment of manual tools. He wasn't a fan of power tools, as he told Emma there is a high chance they'll take off too much of a tooth in a split second. He preferred his old hand tools as he could work more slowly with them and he felt they were less likely to do any damage.

When he came out, we were all brought in together and stood waiting our turns. Conor would work his way along the row. He'd comment on how Wizzy had tartar build up on his canine teeth. This seemed to exasperate his human. She had, it seemed, tried everything to stop it to no avail. He didn't mention any sore spots or damage and the article drifted into my mind. Was he one of the lucky ones?

Conor called Daisy a little princess, which she loved. He filed her teeth, took off any hooks and sharp edges and made a fuss of her. Once again there was no mention of soreness.

I was up next. Conor greeted me warmly and let me sniff about at his tools so I was comfortable before we started. He put the headcollar with the brace on it to hold my teeth open and I ran my tongue over it. It didn't hurt, but it felt odd and a little uncomfortable.

"I know my little man," Conor said fishing a rasp out of his belt. "But has to be done, can't have you chomping down on my arm while I sort these sharp bits out. I'll be quick and you'll feel grand after."

He set to work on my teeth as Emma watched on. She often spoke to me telling me everything was alright and it wouldn't take long. I focused on her voice and tried not to think about the fact someone was filing my teeth. I didn't dislike Conor, and he was right, my teeth did feel better afterwards, but I still didn't enjoy his visits.

"There we are now little man," he said finally letting the cranked sides of the brace down so I could close my mouth again. "Good as new."

Emma smiled. "Conor, while you're here, can I pick your brains a little about bits."

"Sure," he began rinsing his rasps in a bucket of water by my door.

"Well, it's just the vet thinks we may be able to ride soon." My ears perked up, I hadn't known that. A shiver of excitement caused through me. I loved the idea of riding with Emma.

"And, well, I'm not sure what to do. I don't know what bit is best for Lir, or if I even want to use a bit at all. I've been reading up a lot about bitless bridles."

Conor nodded. "Well, let's see." He ushered Emma over to me and opened my mouth a little so she could see inside.

"Look here, this is where the bit will sit. You've plenty of room for one, and his palate is high so you could try a snaffle. Let me just run my thumbs over the bars in his mouth. OK perfect, they're not sharp. Do you want to feel? Just put your thumbs into Lir's mouth, and feel along where the bit would lie on both sides of his mouth."

Emma gently put her thumbs into my mouth and moved them along my bars.

"The bars don't feel sharp," Emma said.

"Exactly," said Conor. "If even one bar felt sharp under your thumb, you wouldn't be able to use any type of jointed bit or snaffle on Lir. When you pick up the reins on a jointed bit, some pressure gets applied to the bars of the horse's mouth. And if one or both bars are sharp, you have a piece of metal applying pressure onto skin over a sharp bone. That's going to cause pain. But anyone can check if their horse has sharp bars, which is great. And there are solutions too – you could try a different bit. Something like a straight bar bit would allow the horse to lift the whole bit up from the bars, to relieve the pressure on his sharp bars if he needed to.

Now, let me show you something else." He took her next door to Wizzy and opened his mouth.

"You see how shallow his palate is?" Emma nodded. "That's the Arab in him, lots of Arabs have shallow palates. You put a single jointed snaffle in there and pick up on the reins, and the nut in the middle will jab the roof of his mouth. That's why he has the French link with a double joint. He wouldn't be comfortable with a single jointed bit."

Emma nodded. "That's so interesting," she said. "So, what would you do with Lir?"

He smiled and glanced at me. "I think I might give the bitless a go, but get an eggbutt snaffle as well. Some showing classes and such don't let you compete without one."

"Oh, we aren't competing, just riding out together," Emma smiled.

"Right now, yes, but one day, who knows, maybe you'll be taking your riding exams on this guy," he ruffled my forelock.

"It would be an interesting experience also to see how Lir goes in both a bitless and a bitted bridle. I've read studies that show that any pressure on the tongue from a bit actually reduces how well their hind legs can move. But when you think about it, the tongue is actually connected to the hindquarters – through the hyoid bone, and then the muscles and fascia, so when you restrict a horse's tongue it's going to impact their whole body. "

Emma nodded, I wanted to nod too. Humans often had no idea how much of a negative effect that pressure on a bit can have on every part of our body.

"Thanks Conor," Emma smiled rubbing my neck. "I think I'm going to give bitless a go."

Chapter 27

The vet, whose name I learnt was James, came out one damp day to 'see how I was doing'. I already knew I was feeling better. I could breathe easily and I'd done a lot of walks now with Wizzy down the little track. Besides, I'd done a few little canters around the field too, just to see if I could. I'd been worried my lungs would feel tight and burning again, but although I quite quickly found myself getting hot and out of puff, it was clearly more because I wasn't as fit as I had been, rather than because my lungs were damaged.

James confirmed my conclusions. He checked me over fully, taking my pulse and checking how my lungs sounded with his little cold stethoscope. I did a trot up and then he had Emma take me into the school on a lunge line.

"I know you don't lunge," he said to Emma.

"It's not my favourite thing, and it's not the best for the horse's joints either but I need to check him over after he's moved a bit, so, we'll go with it. Let's have him walk around a little first, warm up, check him, and then we'll do a few faster circles and check him again. Ok?"

"Ok," Emma seemed nervous. I realised she seemed both excited and worried in equal measure. I understood how she felt because I felt the same. I thought I was doing much better, I hoped James would tell us we could ride, and I was worried I was wrong.

I took a deep breath of fresh, slightly damp, air and set out on my circle. I walked out doing the circles James and Emma asked of me. James checked me over with a smile, and I trotted. James did a much more thorough check after that. Finally, after what seemed to me like hours, he stood back, wrapping his stethoscope around his neck.

"Well," he said with a sigh before a smile broke over his face. "I'd say his lungs are pretty much healed. You need to take it slow, build his fitness, but I see no reason why he can't be ridden again."

A smile spread over Emma's face and she wrapped her arms around my neck. "You hear that, Lir? We can ride! We can go out for hacks with Wizzy - proper ones!"

The next day was a Saturday. We were supposed to go for one of our walks with Wizzy. Emma brought me in as usual, brushed me to perfection, and then appeared with a sidepull bitless bridle she had borrowed. As she adjusted it I realised how much more comfortable it was than my usual bridle.

She took a step back and inspected it. The bridle felt different than when John put my old bridle on, but when Emma gently put a little pressure on one rein to move me over, I understood what she wanted me to do. It was like the groundwork exercises I had done many years ago with Lucy. Emma placed a bareback pad over where my saddle would usually go and fastened the girth around me.

I could sense an excitement in Emma, but she stayed calm and gently led me out of the stables to the little mounting block. I was surprised too. Were we really going to go on a hack? She pulled her riding hat on and slowly climbed up the mounting block. She let me stand next to it giving me scratches until she was sure I was comfortable, then slowly she slid over onto my back.

Emma was lighter than John. She settled into place and I waited patiently. It almost felt strange to have someone on me again, but my focus was on my bridle, not a bit. I liked it. It was comfortable and freeing. I decided I was going to prove to Emma that I liked being ridden this way. Wizzy came out, and after his usual three walks around the mounting block to get straight and close enough for his 'mum' to get on, we set off down the track.

"Urgh," his mum sighed. "If I could only turn back the clock and never have got you that three thousand euro saddle," she said to him, patting his neck when she was settled on board. "You live and learn I guess." She looked over at Emma.

I asked Wizzy what his mum meant. He explained that she once paid a lot of money for someone to make him a custom fitted saddle. The problem was that it had been too tight for his shoulders and made his back hurt. For a while he'd hated being ridden so much that he had even started to buck. His mum realised what was wrong and discovered that he actually needed to wear a wide saddle. After a new saddle, some rest and physio work the pain went away.

"Is that why you don't stand by the mounting block first time?" I asked him as we set off.

Wizzy nodded. "I know it won't hurt. She always checks it fits perfectly before every ride, and also checks my back for any pain or sensitivity after every ride, but it's like I can't help myself," he admitted. I understood what he meant. Someone had burnt some tree trimmings the week before and the smell of the smoke had sent shivers down my spine.

I loved riding bitless. I loved the hack. I wanted to jog and trot, but whenever I tried Emma would say 'whoa' and ask me to just walk. So I did. Finally, I thought, finally I was riding with Emma!

Chapter 28

Over the next few weeks and months, I grew fitter and fitter. Emma and I went from walking slowly down the track with Wizzy to trotting and cantering too. Short rides turned into longer ones and we began to do some schooling under saddle, as well as in-hand. I loved it. All of it. Every day I felt like I soared a little higher, that my life was a little better. With Emma I began to feel like I did when I was young and free with my mother and Nana, like I had been with Lucy. I was happy and content. I had friends in the field to play with, to graze with and to pass the days with. Our paddocks were well maintained and always full of enough grass to keep us happy and healthy.

Sometimes, as I watched the sun set over our paddock, its golden rays stretching over our little bank, turning the stone wall golden rather than grey, I'd think of my old friends.

Was Hamish still happy with Chloe? I had no doubt that barring some illness or frailty he would be, Chloe would never let it be any other way. He was her Hamish, as long as life deemed it so. I was less certain about Seamus and Shannon. They were like I had been, commodities, useful when they were alright, but disposable if anything went wrong. And what were the chances they'd be as lucky as I had been, that if things went wrong for them, they would find an Emma?

I wouldn't have been so lucky if it hadn't been for Chloe vetting anyone who thought to come and see me. I hated thinking those thoughts, they made my heart sink. Worse was if I caught the scent of smoke though, that sent me straight back to the barn and the sounds of King. It still does, though the sounds in my head have faded with time.

The year whizzed by. I focused as much as I could on pleasing Emma, on listening to her and learning to follow her lead. I could tell by her movements, the shift of her weight on my back which way we were to go, how fast, and responded accordingly. We acted like one.

Emma took me new places too, but I enjoyed these outings much more than I had the competitions I had been to with John. Oscar's human had a horsebox, and would take him to the beach sometimes, or on fun rides. There was always room on the horsebox, and so Emma and I began to tag along.

The first time I was nervous, worried I was being dragged back into the world of competitions. I felt an odd sensation in my stomach as I stepped onto the horsebox, expecting the awful rolling motion. Oscar must have noticed my nerves.

"Are you alright?" he asked.

"I don't like the wobbly feel of the horsebox," I admitted shifting my weight and bracing myself for the movement.

"Oh, well, this box isn't so bad," Oscar replied pulling some hay from his net. "It's lower and it doesn't rock much."

He was right. The little horsebox didn't roll quite as much as Alison's larger one. I began to feel a little more at ease as we drove along.

"Where are we going?" I asked Oscar when I realised, I didn't need to constantly worry about stumbling. "Is it jumping? Or a show?"

"A show!" Oscar gave a wicker of a chuckle. "It's a lovely sunny day, why would we go to a show? Nope, today is a beach day."

"A beach day?"

"You've never been on a beach day?"

"I have!" I said. "When I was young we followed the sheep out of our paddock and down to the beach. I remember wading into the water and splashing in the waves. Then my friends and I went cantering in the sand. I loved it!"

And I loved this new beach too. I loved the sinky sand under my hooves once again. I loved the firmer sand by the shore where we could canter and splash in the surf and I loved the sea. It was hot I remember, so very warm, that the cool wetness of the salty water seemed heavenly after a race along the beach. I waded out until the water reached my stomach. Emma squealed and laughed a little as the cool water lapped up her legs. Oscar showed me how to dig in the water, making splashes erupt around us, and causing our humans to laugh even more.

When I look back over my life, that moment in the sea is one of my favourite memories. Warm, loved, happy and having wonderful fun.

We stayed on the beach until the sun dipped a little in the sky. I could have stayed there forever. It was perfect. As we loaded back into the horsebox I glanced back at the ocean with its gentle lapping waves. I came from horses who were brave and strong, horses who came from the sea.

We went to other places that summer too. Long distance rides around woodland or through the green Irish fields sprinkled with ruined castles and fairy forts. We'd come home tired, exhausted even, both me and Emma, but we came back happy. Outings with Emma were fun. There was no pressure, no expectation. All we did was go and be free. We cantered when we wanted, we walked if it was hot and we trotted in the shade of the trees.

It's a strange thing to say that I felt free. I suppose I wasn't, not really. I had to go to the paddock, I was taken to the rides, but I was as free as a horse can be without being wild. I came to consider Emma my partner and my friend, not an owner. She was like my family. That's what she said too. She would hug me goodnight, and always, always told me I was her best friend. She wasn't free either, she had to go to school, as I had to go to the field. When we rode together, then there was nothing, no one but us and nature. When we rode, we were in charge of our actions, our direction, we were free, and I think, no, I'm certain we both felt the same way.

Around Christmas that year Emma came in to the stables with a small white envelope. We had started to come in at night for it had grown bitterly cold and our water trough had frozen solid. Emma opened the envelope and pulled out a card with a horse in a Santa hat on it. It took me a moment to realise the horse was in fact Hamish. He looked happy, if a little silly in the hat. Emma pinned it onto my stable door.

"It's for you," she smiled, rubbing my forehead. She opened it a little. "It says to my hero Lir, happy Christmas from Chloe, Hamish, Shannon and Seamus."

They were OK. I felt relief wash over me. I couldn't have asked for a better gift, though I had already gotten one I suppose, in the form of Emma. On Christmas morning that year she appeared with a small sock stuffed with apples, carrots, and horse treats too. I'd never experienced this before, which surprised Wizzy. He said it was what humans did on Christmas. I didn't have the heart to tell him that most horses I had met would not be given presents from their human on Christmas morning. This year though, I was one of those horses who did.

Chapter 29

My school work with Emma was always fun, both riding and in-hand, but as I got more confident with it, she found new ways to keep me focused and amused. My favourite was the pink circle. I'd never seen one before, but I was very interested in the round, thin, plastic circle Emma appeared with one morning. It was sparkly with a little band of pink. Wizzy didn't like it at all and snorted at it, but it reminded me of some of the jump fillers they'd used at Alison's.

We took it into the outdoor school and Emma set me free, leaning the pink plastic circle against the fence while she closed the gate and fastened it shut. I took the opportunity to examine it more closely, I nudged it with my nose and it rolled a little making me snort. But seeing that Emma had been carrying it not so long ago, I was pretty sure it wouldn't hurt me. I put my nose on it again, and then picked it up in my mouth tossing it up and down as I walked and trotted around the school with it.

Emma laughed so hard I think she cried a little. "That's not what we're using it for."

I stopped and looked at her, the pink plastic circle drooping in my mouth. She walked up and gently took it from me shaking her head with a smile.

Emma placed the pink plastic circle on the ground and had me put my front two feet in it. I wasn't sure what we were doing, but she asked me to move my hind feet leaving my front ones stationary in the circle. It took a few attempts for me to fully understand what she was asking, but when I did, she was very happy. That made me happy.

Emma would also put poles out and ask me to step sideways over them, and take a few steps backwards. Sometimes I did this as an individual movements, sometimes together. On our hacks I realised this helped me a great deal when opening and closing gates, especially tricky ones.

Our ridden work came on too. I started to anticipate what Emma was going to ask me simply by the way she moved, her weight change and position. I knew when she was looking in a direction and that it meant we'd be going that way. One evening we shared the school with Wizzy and his mum. She was sat with long loopy reins twisting her shoulders in the direction she was looking and encouraging Wizzy to turn without any rein signals. Emma asked her about it and she explained it was something she did in lessons, trying to get Wizzy to move without any reins. She suggested Emma give it a shot.

I remember being a little worried when Emma let go of the reins, she tied them in a knot that flopped onto my shoulder. Her weight was the same though, and as soon as she shifted her line of sight, I understood. I turned and she patted me enthusiastically.

"That's amazing!"

"I know," Wizzy's mum said. "Sometimes we don't realise how smart our horses are!"

We practised it a lot after that. I grew to like it a lot. Sometimes we'd work on collection. I found this hard at first. When I'd worked at Alison's there had been a focus on what John called impulsion, getting momentum to pop over fences. Emma was more focused on improving my posture so that I put a little less weight on my front legs and a little more weight on my hind legs. She explained as we rode around, that with a rider on board, carrying too much weight on my two front legs wasn't good for my body.

So she would ask me to gently bend my body a little like the circle we were riding on, and then to step just my inside hind foot underneath my body a bit more. But I was never asked to tuck my nose in as I had often been asked to do before.

I soon understood that when my inside hind leg stepped under my body more deeply, my body felt lighter and stronger, that way everything was nice and evenly distributed. Once I got the hang of it, and started to feel my muscles grow stronger, it felt amazing. I felt so athletic!

Emma also started to ask me to do something called shoulder out. I had to walk along the fence line and look to the outside a little. When we did it, my hooves were on three tracks, and my hind hoof beside the fence, had to step underneath my body a little deeper than normal. It also really helped my muscles to feel stronger and made me feel more balanced!

I couldn't help but be enthusiastic about it all in the field with Wizzy, Daisy and Oscar. I felt more supple and strong, more than I ever had. It had been good enough not to feel broken after my burnt lungs, but now I didn't just feel fixed, I felt fit and healthy.

"We're lucky," Oscar said as he munched on some hay. "Most humans don't understand how to do those kinds of exercises, or what they can do for us."

"It's true," Daisy nodded. "Oscar's human had special lessons to learn them. Then she showed them to the humans here. She even showed Emma some, although that girl's read a ton more since."

"All humans should be taught them," Oscar stated. "Make them better riders."

"Maybe they will be," Wizzy mused. "After all, isn't that what Emma hopes to do? Teach people?"

I liked that thought. One day maybe my Emma would teach other riders how to treat their horses as well as she treats me. Yes, I liked that idea a lot.

Oscar's human was a member of the local horse riding club. They were the people who organised all of the fun long-distance rides we went on, but they also held a small show and a couple of dressage competitions throughout the year. Emma wasn't interested in competing, but since the horse riding club donated all the profits to horse charities, she decided we should go along with Oscar and his human.

There was no pressure on me. It was a different feeling than it had been with Alison. I knew wherever

Emma took me, she went for fun. I had nothing to prove to her. In her eyes I was perfect. So, when I stepped off the horsebox at our first little dressage meet, I felt rather good. There was a buzz about the place, but it was happy and friendly. I knew almost all the assembled horses and ponies from other outings. People chatted and laughed, no one seemed too serious or focused. It was a jolly day out, just like the long-distance rides.

When it was our turn to do the little test, Emma gave me a pat and simply said. "We'll do our best. It's all for less fortunate ponies, not rosettes."

Any remaining nerves melted away and we walked into the little school. There was a lady sat in a red car at the far end. She tooted the horn, just once and off we went. Emma and I had practised the test a few times, enough for me to know exactly where we'd turn, where we'd trot and where we'd canter. I focused not on my surroundings, not on the test, but on Emma, on my balance and listening to what she wanted.

I knew we must have done well when we came out because Wizzy's mum was there saying how well we'd done and how lovely I'd looked. She snuck me a treat, but I know Emma knew about it from the grin she gave me.

There were some fields we could hack about while we waited for our turns, or after we had done our tests and Emma and I went off for a walk around them. It was nice being alone together somewhere new. When I came back I saw Oscar's human grinning at us. She held up a blue rosette.

"You two came second," she smiled.

"Hear that Lir," Emma hugged me. "We were second." We. I thought happily. Not I, we were second.

Chapter 30

That first dressage outing for fun led to more outings with the horse riding club, and I actually enjoyed them. Emma never went to win; she went to have fun and meet up with some of the friends we made. They were always close to the yard, little short trips, so even going on the horsebox was nicer.

We began to jump together in the spring. Starting with small cross poles in the school. At first, I thought I'd hate it, that it would mean I went back to my old life, but then I remembered I was with Emma. Jumping with her was fun. She never pushed me, never did it day after day. It was just another facet of life that dropped in. Another, different thing to do to keep my mind focused. Sometimes we even jumped out in the fields, sometimes over poles, sometimes over rustic fences, logs, ditches, and little walls. I liked that a lot.

Soon we began to jump little things when we were out on the long-distance rides. I had noticed that there was often a little fence here or there as an option on the trails, but I'd never been allowed to do them until now.   I sometimes got a little excited doing the outdoor fences, but when I did Emma would slow everything down until I calmed and we'd try again.

I began to love jumping. Perhaps it was because I could do it again, proof that my lungs were alright, that I was, well, me again. I could fly. I think though, it was more that for the first time I was jumping with someone who jumped with me for fun, for the thrill of it, and not to prove anything. If I knocked over a pole, or took my time, it didn't matter. It was a new way of jumping, and it was much nicer than it had been.

At the little shows the horse riding club put on we started doing working hunter classes and a few small show jumping ones.   Emma liked the little clear round courses and I liked the working hunter. They made show jumps out of natural looking things for us to jump. Little fake hedges made of jump fillers filled with brush, tyre jumps and hay bales. They were my favourite. We began to do well in the hunter classes. Apparently, I was not only good at jumping, I was good at moving too. I did well in the showing part of the hunter classes, and even better at the little dressage competitions. We got a few rosettes to add to our first one too. Soon we had a rainbow of coloured ribbons fastened to my door. Emma always took a picture of me wearing them.

She showed me them one day. She brought a big book to the yard filled with photos of us. Some I had rosettes on and we were dressed up for shows, some were pictures Oscar's human took of us on long distance rides in front of castles or in woods. There were pictures of me grazing in the field and photos of me and Wizzy on a ride. My favourite though was one of us on the beach. We were in the shallows, me pawing at the water and sending it flying. Emma was sitting on me bareback laughing. It summed us up perfectly.

One of the shows we attended I won the hunter class. Emma was very proud of me, of us. She hugged me as she pinned the little red ribbon on my bridle. The judge was a smiling woman in a smart hat. She came over as we left the ring.

"I have to say, you both did a very good job today. I think you could do very well in dressage, or even eventing," she smiled at Emma, focusing more on her than me.

I felt put out at that. I realised I had come to see myself as an equal part of a team. It was me and Emma, together equally, the annoyance I felt gave way to joy. In a way the judge's comments had revealed to me just how much had changed in my life, how much my perception of myself and of humans, at least some humans, had altered since I came to live with Emma.

I'll never forget Emma's answer to that judge. She turned and smiled at me, moving a few stray strands of grey forelock out of my eyes.

"I'm not interested in competing. I don't need proof Lir's the best," she turned back to the judge with a smile. "I hope to take my test on him though."

"You're planning on becoming an instructor?" the judge asked.

Emma nodded. "I want to teach people how to ride in harmony with their horses."

"An admirable goal," the judge smiled and I saw a hint of something on her face, she lent in closer. "Something more riders should aspire too."

I realised then that this woman, this human, I may have misjudged. She had spoken to Emma not knowing us, not knowing Emma that thought of me so highly. The judge patted my neck.

"I think he would be an excellent partner to get you through your examinations," she said. "If memory serves me correctly, you would need to jump just a little higher than today's course, but I'd say he's more than capable of that. Yes, I should think you'd do just fine."

She walked away from us still smiling and I nuzzled into Emma. I loved the thought that I could be part of her journey to teaching other humans the kind way to ride and train horses. Emma understood us, understood we were individuals, and understood that it was always ok to find out you were doing something wrong, so long as you put it right.

She never stopped trying to learn new things, new kinder ways, and putting them into practise. I loved Emma not because she was perfect, but because she was perfect for me. We fit together, and I knew she would always, always do everything she could to help me.

Chapter 31

I thought my life would be glorious forever. Everything was perfect. I was happy, and content. I was with Emma, I had friends and I was fit and healthy again. I was even enjoying jumping and doing a few little shows. I was settled and I felt safe, but I had forgotten one thing. Emma didn't own me, Alison did. My safe life was built on unstable foundations and I had forgotten it in the joy of everything going on in my life.

One morning Alison showed up to see me. I was surprised to see her, but it seemed like Emma had expected her to come. She seemed happy to welcome her and talk about me, and I was happy to see Chloe who came skipping over and gave me a hug. She perched herself on the wall and started telling me all about the things she and Hamish were doing. I only partly heard what she said though because I was watching Emma, and I saw her face fall. One moment she was happy and smiling and telling Alison all about what we had been up to, the next she looked as if someone had poured cold water on her.

She looked over at me and I knew something was wrong. Very, very wrong.

Alison checked me over and saw me do some work, but the whole time I knew something was looming over us. Emma was not her usual self. She was quiet and withdrawn. She felt tense when we rode too. I could feel it through the saddle, and once Alison left, she broke down crying. Wizzy's mum came over asking if she was alright and she shook her head crying harder. I watched as Wizzy's mum hugged her asking her what was going on.

It took Emma nearly five minutes before she could speak. When she did I knew why she had been so off all day. Alison was selling up her yard, everything, and downsizing to a small farm with only a couple of stables. Hamish was safe, but the rest of us were to be sold. Seamus, Shannon, and I.

"I'd buy him in a heartbeat," Emma sobbed. "I've been saving up in case this happened, but I only have half of what she wants."

"But, you'd give him a great home," Wizzy's mum said with a smile. "He's happy here! Will she not take less?"

Emma shook her head. "I asked her, she said she needs more."

"Oh honey, I'm so sorry," Wizzy's mum glanced at me sadly.

"You could ask your mum," Daisy's little girl said, as she wandered past almost completely obscured by her tack.

"Ask me what? Sweetie, what's wrong?" Emma's mum stepped into the stables.

Wizzy's mum gave Emma a nod and then left us alone. Emma looked over at her mum and sniffled.

"Alison came by," she admitted. "She's giving up the jumping yard. She said she took a big hit with the barn fire, and things didn't go well this season. She decided to sell up the yard and move into a farm she inherited from her aunt. She's only keeping Chloe's ponies. She wants to sell the rest, including Lir." Emma glanced at me.

"Oh sweetheart," her mum hugged her.

"I can't afford him mum," Emma cried. "I saved as much as I can, but I can't afford him."

"Sweetheart, I'm sorry. I know you love Lir, but he isn't ours." She looked at me kindly. "You can keep saving, maybe get your own horse after you finish your education."

"No!" Emma looked horrified. "No, there'll never be another Lir. And I need him. I need him to do my instructor tests. This is what I want to do with my life!"

"I know," her mum nodded. "And if I had the money I'd give you it, but I don't sweetheart." She sighed. "Look, why don't you give Alison a ring and ask her if you can pay in instalments or something?"

It was a long shot and I knew it. I think Emma knew it too, but it was all we had to cling onto. Emma lingered in the stables that night, not wanting to leave me, as if she was soaking up every second with me.

That night, after she was gone, I stood alone in the darkness of the paddock feeling lost. Suddenly my safe field, my safe life with Emma, was under threat. Once again humans were deciding my fate, and it looked certain I was going to move again, be torn away from my human, the one who loved me and who I loved. It seemed wrong, so very wrong.

Wizzy, Oscar and Daisy grazed around me happily, seemingly oblivious to the impending end of the world. Did Shannon and Seamus know? What would happen to them? What would happen to me? If I had to leave Emma where would I go? Where would I end up? Who would care for me? Would they be like Emma?

No, they wouldn't be like Emma, they couldn't be like Emma, no one could. No human could ever be Emma. My Emma. I felt my heart breaking and what was worse I knew hers was too. She didn't want me to go. She wanted me with her forever. We were being torn apart and we couldn't stop it.

I looked out over the dark field and wondered if we could just go out on a ride and never come back, run away together over the fields wild and free. I knew we couldn't, but I so wished we could.

I didn't sleep at all that night, every time I closed my eyes, I saw Emma's tearstained face. I think that night I hated Alison, I'd disliked humans before, but not like this. Alison could have let me stay with Emma, but she wouldn't, she wouldn't because she wanted money. My life to her meant nothing, my happiness meant nothing. All she really cared about was the money. Once again I had been reduced to being a commodity, a thing, with no feelings.

Chapter 32

The next couple of weeks were tense. Our happy existence had been shattered. People began to come out to see me. Everyone that did made Emma upset. Some were kind, others not as much. Either way it didn't matter, they weren't Emma. She was who I wanted, and she wanted me. I watched her cry when the visitors left, or at least look heartbroken.

I began to worry that every day together would be our last. Every morning I'd wait for Emma hoping that this wouldn't be the day we were separated, that we could have just one more day together, but I knew time was running out. I even tried being a little naughty for some of the viewers, but if they were children, I couldn't bring myself to do it. I looked at them and thought of Chloe.

Emma spent a lot of time looking for a way for us to stay together. She looked for jobs to earn extra money, looked into colleges nearby so she could study and stay at home hoping it would mean her mum or dad could find the extra cash for me. I know she even tried asking Alison if she could buy me and pay her in instalments. I didn't know what that meant, but Oscar did, his human had bought their horsebox that way. It meant to pay in little chunks. Alison didn't want to do that though, she wanted me sold. She wanted rid of me, and she wanted it for the highest price she could get.

I always knew humans came in as many varieties as horses, but at this point in my life I learnt an interesting thing. Horses, by nature are compassionate creatures, all of us, humans are not. There are those who are, but many who are selfish, thinking only of their wants and needs. I was learning that fast.

You only have to look at a horse meeting a human who is young, or perhaps in some way injured, they will become instantly gentle.

I watched a video on Emma's phone once. It was of one of the big black horses that guards the royal palace in London. A young boy in a wheelchair was taken to get his picture taken. The horse was standing still looking unhappy, ears back, tail swishing, but when he noticed the boy, he instantly changed, sidling closer to him and lowering his head for a fuss. Horses are better than people Emma sometimes said. Wizzy's mum would laugh when she said it and would nod her head but add, most horses are better than most people. I think she might have been right.

Wizzy, Oscar and Daisy all tried to comfort me as the parade of new humans came to the yard. They would say things like don't give up hope, or at least this one or that one didn't seem too bad. I knew they meant well but it didn't help. I felt as if I was being herded towards a cliff edge with no way to go.

Then, one morning, it happened. Emma came down looking awful. Her face was pale, her eyes red rimmed from crying and I knew, I knew as soon as I looked at her. She didn't say a word, just came over to me, wrapped her arms around my neck and said she was sorry. She explained how she had tried her best and failed. She cried, sobbing into my neck until I could feel the dampness though my thick coat. This was it then, someone had offered Alison enough money for me and she had taken it.

It was the worst moment of my life. I had everything, everything, and it was all going to be taken away from me. Worse, it was being taken away not by Emma, not by me, not even by fate. It was being done by another human who showed no compassion to Emma, and no care or regard for me. I was, to Alison, the same as her horsebox, her car, her saddle, I was just an object. To Emma and Chloe

I was a living soul with thoughts, feelings, and dreams, I was prized, honoured and loved for being who I was. To Alison I was a thing worth money. I had no feelings, things can't feel, can they? I was prized for sure, but it was for what I could do for her, for the money I could bring her, for the glory or the prestige, nothing more.

I began to panic. Where was I going this time? Without Emma life seemed meaningless, hopeless, worthless. We were a team, part of each other. Who would I be with now? What would life be like? I knew I'd never feel with them like I did with Emma. I suddenly realised it would almost have been better if Emma hadn't wanted me, because the pain of knowing she did but we couldn't be together was almost unbearable. I was heartbroken and so was she.

We went out for a ride that day. Our last one together at our little home. We went down the track and through the little corner of trees at the bottom of it. We rode in silence. I don't think Emma could speak. Every time she did fresh tears flowed from her blue eyes.

When we got back and she untacked me and pulled herself up and sniffed. She took my head in her hands gently and placed her forehead on mine.

"I'm going to keep tabs on you, check you're alright. I promise. The girl," her voice hitched. "The woman who bought you seems nice, she likes to event," she tried to smile, but it failed. "And, it's a big yard, so that's nice, I suppose, you'll have lots of friends. I don't, I don't think this will be your forever home I'm afraid."

I flicked my ears. I knew what that meant. Wizzy told me. His mum was his forever home, she never sold on. Ever. It was her mantra he said. If she took on a horse it was like a marriage, till death do you part, in sickness and in health. She'd rather live on bread and jam than let him go. I knew Emma would be the same one day. "I promise I won't forget you," she said hugging me. "Please don't forget me."

As if I would. As if I could. My Emma, my whole world. I would never forget her, or what she had done for me.

The next morning a horsebox came for me and at the age of 12 I was torn away from what I had dreamed was my forever home. A young woman got out with a bright smile.

I remembered them vaguely, the woman had soft hands. She had led me around a little, and ridden while another woman watched me move. She seemed happy, a huge grin on her face as she looked at me and patted me on the neck. I snuggled into Emma. I knew why I was going, but I still couldn't quite understand how we could be torn apart, how she couldn't stop it somehow. The woman took the rope out of Emma's hands and led me up the ramp. I kept looking back at Emma, shouting to tell her how much I cared. She began to cry again and Wizzy's mum put her arm around her, pulling her into a hug. I kept my eyes on her right up until the ramp closed, shutting the image of her away.

Chapter 33

I learnt that the girl who had collected me was called Laura. She was a cheerful person who sang along to music as we drove back to what would be my new home. Her cheerfulness was in stark contrast to my own feelings. I don't think I had ever felt so alone.

My new home was a large eventing yard in Cork. It was the centre of the world according to Shannon. I wondered if that was true. Laura took me off the horsebox and led me to a nice comfortable stable, putting me inside with a hay net and fresh water. The journey had left me sweating and she sponged me down a little and put on a cooler to keep me warm.

"There we go, you're grand now" she smiled. Another horse somewhere on the yard shouted hearing her voice. "All right, I'm coming." She glanced at me. "Must be din-din time, eh?" she rubbed my neck. "Everyone wants their tea."

I soon discovered that Laura was one of the three yard staff that worked on the yard. The others were a girl called Ana, and a twenty-year-old man they called Don, which I found out was short for Donal. These two, unlike Laura, didn't treat us as individuals with feelings. We were something to be moved, cleaned and fed, but there was no affection. Once again, I was a commodity.

My feed was slowly changed. It went from lots of hay with a few cob nuts, to a half a bucket of hard feed with oats and cereals every day. Life changed too. The freedom of the paddocks and hacks with Emma was replaced with a regimented routine. The same time every morning I was fed, then rugged and turned out in order. If Laura came for me, she'd chat to me as she took me to the paddock, telling me whatever was going on in life. I liked that. Ava and Don wouldn't say a word if they fetched me. Don would even take several of us at once if he could get away with it so he could be done with his chores faster.

The yard was worked in two halves. I was on the afternoon schedule. At lunch time I was brought into a cleaned stable, given a hay net and brushed by one of the staff. Laura would inspect every inch of me for cuts and scrapes, though Don and Ava were less thorough. After that I was tacked up and taken to train or exercise. Several different riders would exercise me. Some did dressage. Some took me to jump in the school, others out to a little gallops where we trained over rustic cross country fences. I didn't feel a connection with any of them, and I slowly began to dislike jumping once again. The numb feeling I'd had at the yard with Alison reared its head again, I could feel it creeping in.

I hated the unevenness of my life. The routine I could cope with, the lack of connection I couldn't. I felt lost and alone. I barely saw my owner, the woman who had actually bought me from Alison. She came mostly at weekends to practice her eventing with me, but she didn't stay long after our rides and I never saw her during the week unless she had an extra lesson planned.

Often, I ran out of hay overnight and felt hungry too. It made me feel even more anxious. Sometimes Laura would do lockup, coming around and checking all the doors were bolted. She'd always check our hay and slip me more if I looked low, but it was usually Don's job and he never bothered to look.

I pined for Emma, thinking about her alone in my stable. I thought about what life had been, but it hurt to do so, it made my present situation seem ten times worse. I wondered what she was doing too. Was she alright? Was she missing me? Was she riding still? Who was she riding? Without me could she, would she become an instructor?

Every thought of Emma made me feel horrible. I missed her so much, but when I thought about her my heart broke. I started to stop thinking about anything, trying to block out everything. Slowly I shut down, blocking out the world.

A few weeks after I arrived at the yard, I met Murphy. He'd been away at a competition and had come back with a slight injury so had been on box rest. He was a large grey Irish Draught with a happy attitude and pleasant manner. He was getting older now, in fact he was the oldest horse on the yard, but he still competed and did quite well it seemed. His owner, and rider, was a girl called Bridget. She wasn't that much older than Emma, and seeing her with Murphy made me instantly jealous. Bridget came to the yard every day, brushed, rode, and cared for him. It made me dislike Murphy in the beginning.

Slowly though I began to warm to him, how could I not. Murphy was sweet, kind, and gentle. He liked everyone, including me, even when I was grumpy. He'd chat to me, ask questions, and broke down my barriers. I eventually told him all about Emma.

He instantly understood why I felt so lost, and unfriendly towards him, but he didn't pity me, which I was thankful for. Instead of consoling me, telling me how sorry he was for us being separated, he told me not to block out the memories of Emma, he told me to cling to them, to use them to get me through the bad days. He had been around the block several times and felt as I did, but he was confident that Bridget would keep him safe and not give him up. He was not a commodity, at least not anymore. I hoped, for his sake, he was right.

We spent a lot of time together after that. A lot of the younger horses were too much for Murphy, running around and play fighting. I on the other hand liked to stand and graze and chat. We fitted well together.

At least now, I thought, in Murphy I had a friend. Someone to talk with, to express my feelings to. Someone who would stop me from completely losing myself in the black numbness that threatened to engulf me. Murphy and Laura. They were the ones who kept me going during my time at that yard. If it wasn't for them I may well have shut down completely and lost myself in the process.

Chapter 34

My new owner was called Siobhan. She had been competing for some time, I was not her first equine partner, and I was certain I would not be the last. She was not a bad rider, her hands were light enough and she didn't kick or pull at me. But I could not find a rhythm with her. She didn't ride like Emma or like the riders from the yard who exercised me during the week. It made competing hard. I struggled with our flow in the dressage and with my strides in jumping. I didn't dislike her, but I didn't care about her either.

Still, we began to compete. At first it was local, no further than the horse riding club rides I'd gone on with Oscar. It was fine. Not great, but fine. I could manage the journeys and I could easily do what was asked of me, though I did so with little enthusiasm. Often Murphy went too, which at least gave me company.

Most of the competitions we went to I was prepped by the yard staff, and they were there to see to me afterwards too. This stood in stark contrast to

Murphy, who was always seen to by Bridget. It made me sad for myself, but happy at least for my friend.

Murphy would go to bigger competitions too, and soon enough Siobhan was taking me to them as well. It meant longer journeys. She didn't like that I sweated as I travelled, nor that it took me a little to settle when we arrived at our destination, but mostly she shrugged it off. Certainly, she never tried to rectify the issue, or even try to work out what bothered me. If anything, Bridget seemed to care more. She'd suggest things that could help me when I travelled, but Siobhan would just shake her head and say I needed to get used to it.

I tried to think back to Nana's words, to try hard, and I focused on doing my job as best I could. I felt awkward and uncomfortable with Siobhan, but we must have done alright and looked good enough to the judges, because we seemed to do fairly well. Any prizes won though were for the glory of Siobhan, we were certainly not a team. No ribbons adorned my door, no real praise came my way. I was petted and patted after a good round, but it was all for show, for the crowd of spectators, not for me, not really.

Laura would always slip me extra carrots after an event and give me an extra pat and a hug or a scratch telling me how well I'd done and how clever I was. I shared her with a whole yard of horses, but to this day I hope, somehow, deep down, that she knows how much we appreciated that. Her kinds words, her care. It was all some of us got.

Over the course of a long and hot, summer, we competed nearly every weekend. The ground grew harder and I automatically slowed, but Siobhan pushed me to keep going and I tried to do so without hurting myself. Murphy found the heat intolerable. He was already slowing down, but the hard ground and intense heat were taking their toll. Unlike Siobhan, Bridget just went with the flow. This resulted in fewer wins and placements for the pair, while we, Siobhan, and I, continued to do well, and even improved a little.

I will never forget the conversation I overheard between Siobhan and Bridget after one intense cross country trial. It had taken Murphy a lot longer to warm up that day and Bridget was concerned he might be starting to have something called arthritis. I gathered it would mean his joints would ache a little, especially in the cold and the damp.

"If he is getting arthritis," Siobhan said as she packed up some of our equipment into the horsebox. "It'll be an end to competing."

"Maybe," Bridget replied. "We might just have to do smaller competitions."

"You could always get a youngster, bring it on to replace Murphy when he can't do the big stuff anymore," Siobhan shrugged. "It's what I would have done if I hadn't lost Raj young."

I pricked my ears up. So that was her plan. I was her competition horse until I was old, then a younger me would take over, and I would what? I wondered. Maybe retire? Live with Laura just making sure I was ok? It wasn't my preferred life, but it could be worse I mused.

"No," Bridget shook her head. "I can't keep two."

"Oh." Siobhan paused and looked over at Bridget. "Well, in that case I suppose there's only one thing to do. If you want to keep competing the kindest thing is to put Murphy down and get a youngster."

I froze. Put Murphy down. Why would he be put down? Ok he was getting older and stiff, but he was ok, he was healthy. Would a human actually put one of us down just so they could compete? Would Siobhan do that to me?

Bridget looked horrified. "I can't do that to Murphy!"

Siobhan shook her head. "I know it sounds cruel, but it's less cruel than passing on an old horse with problems. Lord knows who would take him on or where he'd end up."

"I know," Bridget looked down.

"Look, remember Amber? Cora's old horse. She put her down rather than sell her on for those very reasons."

Bridget looked up. "Amber was different. She lost her job, had no money, it was a choice of sell on or put down, she was twenty-seven and on two Bute a day. She sobbed for days over that, and she stayed with her the whole time. The vet even said he didn't think Amber had another winter in her."

Siobhan glanced at her as if she didn't understand the difference, but I did. The situations seemed very, very different. Siobhan shrugged.

"Up to you, but if you want to be the best, you can't do it on an arthritic horse."

"Well then I don't want to be the best," Bridget replied.

I didn't realise that Murphy had overheard that conversation until I looked up and saw him peering out of the horse box. He looked very relieved. I would have been too if I were him. Siobhan stepped inside the little day living area with my saddle, while Bridget skipped up the ramp and gave the big grey a hug.

"Don't worry. I'd never do that to you, not unless I absolutely had to. Putting someone down is always a last resort," she smiled at Murphy and moved his forelock a little. "If we can't compete, we won't. If we can't ride, we won't," she smiled.

Murphy, I realised was a very lucky horse. He'd found his forever home. Siobhan hopped out and took hold of my lead rope, taking me to the ramp. I hadn't found my forever home. At least I hoped I hadn't. That moment, that conversation, that was the instant I decided I'd prefer to not grow old with Siobhan. In fact, that was the moment I decided I didn't really like her very much at all.

Chapter 35

The heatwave continued making our competitions harder work for me. We only did one day events meaning I would do all three disciplines, dressage, show jumping and cross country in the space of a day. Some of the events were cancelled, but more tried to work around the heat. They'd start a little earlier, have extra water and cool shady areas for us, and even added sand to the areas in front and behind the fences so it was softer. Still, I was struggling and Siobhan didn't seem to notice, or perhaps she just didn't care.

I stayed in the stable a lot more when we were competing. Siobhan said it was because she wanted to protect me. I knew she meant from injury in the field, since it seemed she cared little about my actual welfare beyond my ability to jump and perform for her. I hated that. Cooped up in the stable, often running out of hay, while the other horses would go out and bask in the sunshine.

One particularly warm morning she turned up and began to get me ready for the day. I noticed

Bridget wasn't there and I overheard Siobhan chatting to Ava saying she'd pulled out that day thinking it was too much for Murphy. Siobhan had shaken her head and Ava had chuckled a little. I on the other hand wished I was Murphy.

The journey to the competition in Meath wasn't short. I hated it. It was bad enough travelling in the horsebox with company, but alone, in the heat, it was unbearable. I felt stiff from bracing myself when Siobhan unloaded me. I was already dreading the return journey when we entered the warm-up ring.

We did alright that day, not brilliantly, but good enough I suppose, Siobhan seemed happy enough. I was exhausted though. The heat, the big fences and the journey made me feel drained. I was right about travelling home too. It was horrible. I felt wobbly and tried desperately to maintain my balance. I could feel the sweat pouring out of me. By the time we got home I was worried I'd collapse on the ramp.

Siobhan didn't seem to notice I was worse than normal travelling back. She sponged off the sweat, threw a cooler on me and put me in my stable with a bucket of feed I wasn't really interested in and went home to take a shower.

My symptoms came on slowly, but intensely none the less. The feeling of tension I'd had on the horsebox didn't dissipate like it usually did. Instead, it got worse. My muscles began to hurt and I shook involuntarily, as if I had no control over them. An observer might have thought I was cold, but I wasn't. I could feel my tail clamp to my rump, my whole back end almost trying to curve under me. A fear, a panic rose in my chest, my heart hammering. What was wrong with me? What was happening?

Flashes of the day flitted through my mind, racing across my memory, and making me feel almost giddy. My breathing became rapid as I fought the adrenaline surging through me, the fear. I couldn't move. I felt frozen, like my limbs weren't mine anymore. If I did try to shift my position pain shot through me, aching thumping pain that made me shake more.

I was alone, scared and something was wrong with me. I wanted Emma. I wanted someone who cared, who would help me, who I could trust. I wanted to call out. A light flicked on and Laura's face popped over the top door of my stable. She looked at me with a smile.

"No night night kiss tonight..." her smile turned to a frown as soon as she looked at me. She unbolted the door and came over a worried look on her face as she scanned me over with searching eyes. Instantly she had her phone out and was dialling.

"Hiya, something is not right with Lir," there was a pause. "Well, he might have been ok then, but he's definitely not now. He needs a vet," I could vaguely make out Siobhan's voice through the speaker. "No, he needs a vet now. Yeah, yeah I'll call, you get yourself sorted, I'll stay with him."

She hung up gave me a smile and then called the vet. I heard her describing my state to them over the phone. "Now then," she soothed me. "The vet's on his way, ok, it'll be alright," she stroked my neck and rubbed my muzzle. "Aunty Laura will stay with you ok? It'll be fine."

She didn't stop speaking to me or fussing me until the vet arrived. I was grateful for that. It was a distraction I badly needed, and a kind interaction when I feared none would come.

The vet was a man I hadn't seen before. He was a tall man called Craig, who originally came from Scotland. He examined me all over, checking my heart rate, my pulse, and asking Laura lots of questions about me. She did her best to answer, but she hadn't been at the competition so didn't know all of the specific details.

"Well," Craig stepped back looking me over. "I'm pretty sure he's tied up. I'll take some bloods to be certain, but I'm pretty sure. I'll give him some pain killers, keep him in a while, and keep him warm, not that it's really a problem in this heat, I'm surprised he has a cooler on."

"I suspect Siobhan forgot to take it off," Laura muttered a little darkly. "What do we need to do to prevent this happening again?"

"He's inside a lot?" Laura nodded. "Once he's over this bout I'd turn him out more. He needs reduced stress and turnout should help that. Other than that, make sure he drinks plenty, and that he has electrolyte balancer if he's competing, especially in heat like this when he sweats more.

Feed wise, go low carbs if you can, if he needs some for competitions just a little for the everyday feed and up it a bit on the day. Selenium can help, and make sure warm up and cool downs are done properly. Not a good idea to leave him too long between work sessions either, at least not if he's doing anything intense. Fine if he's a happy hacker."

Laura looked at him with a sigh.

"Look, in all honesty," she glanced around to make sure we were alone. "I could do with you telling his owner all this, only," she bit her lip, "you might need to put it in terms she'll understand."

"What do you mean?"

She looked at me. "Well, it's better to put it that the recommendations will make sure he's capable of doing his job rather than, you know, making his life better."

Craig nodded. "Oh, she's one of them is she," Laura smiled just a little.

"I'll sort it. Don't you worry." He gave me a pat.

He gave me a shot of something that began to take the pain in my muscles away, and something else to ease my panic. I began to relax, just a little, and by the next morning I felt able to at least move from the back corner of my stable to the front door in order to greet Laura. She promised me Craig had done his job well and Siobhan was on board with how I would be treated going forward. It pleased me that at least she cared about me.

Chapter 36

I had time on my box rest to observe the yard I was on and the horses a little better. Box rest is dull and boring, so people and horse watching became the most interesting way I could spend my time. Laura would move me to a spare stable during the day, one that faced the arena, so I 'had a view' as she put it. My day stall had very little in the way of bedding, just a scattering of shavings over rubber matting, but I liked it anyway.

Lots of the horses I observed from my temporary day time accommodations looked somehow off, uncomfortable in some way, and I wondered why.

There was a particular group that would ride often together, a bevy of girls with big Irish Draughts, a little like Murphy. They all had matching saddles and numnahs, and would go on about how much this or that cost and how much they spent on their horses. Yet, as I watched I observed that the horses always looked slightly stiff, or stunted in their movement. I wondered how their humans couldn't see, or feel it.

I learned the reason these horses moved so strangely from another human. His name was Paddy Morgan.

I remember his name being whispered around the yard excitedly for weeks before his arrival. I listened intently to what the girls on the yard were saying about this mysterious man and learned he was a very well-respected eventing trainer who had once been an international competitor himself.

He apparently 'had an uncanny way with horses' and he was coming to our yard for a weekend. He was there to do workshops, classes, and even some 1-1 training. Though he lived not far away, this was the first time he had ever come to our stables, and there was a herculean effort to make them sparkle and shine.

Siobhan was irritated that the vet hadn't cleared me for full work yet, so she couldn't take part in any of the classes. Unlike her however, I still was determined to watch them. I wanted to know if this human really did have a way with us.

I don't know what I expected Paddy to be like, but it wasn't the 60 year old man with black curly hair, a kind crinkled face and deep tan that showed up one bright morning. While the yard was a buzz of excitement, he remained calm, uninterested in the flashy saddles and was much more focused on the horses. He began by wandering around the stables meeting us all and giving us a gentle rub. When he saw Laura, she led him to my day box. He asked about me and she explained everything.

He looked me over with a smile. "Bit of care and attention," he patted me. "It might be a single occurrence." I hoped he was right.

I watched a group lesson he gave first. An assembled mass of young riders, mostly on ponies gathered in the school. He smiled at them and asked their names, as well as those of their horses.

"Well then, shall we get started?" There was a chorus of yeses and he chuckled. "Ok, well, let's go over some things first. How long would it take to train a horse to carefully and safely jump a sizeable bank or a ditch?"

"A day or two?" a little boy piped up.

Paddy shook his head. "It takes me at least 3 weeks to do it properly, slowly building up, with short sessions and a day or two off between sessions, to give the horse time to think. Often horses seems to learn more in the times between training sessions, rather than during training sessions I find. So I never like to rush a horse. Instead we go slowly and break everything down into little steps. Good horse training is about quality, not speed."

Paddy went on asking questions as he taught. He had the participants do circles, trots and leg yields, helping them if they didn't understand how to do something. His keen eyes watched every horse's movement in great detail. I learned he had two horses of his own, and by the end of that class I wished I was one of them.

"I can only help you improve your flatwork so much today," he said.

"You have to improve it by listening to your horse too. When you do that, you develop a stronger bond. A stronger bond makes a better team, and a better team always works..."

"Better!" the kids chorused and giggled.

He squinted at a girl on a pretty little pony I noticed was wearing a flash noseband which stopped her horse from opening his mouth. I shuddered at the memory of it. He pulled her to one side and asked about it kindly, not making her feel like a bad rider, just as if he were inquisitive.

"She opens her mouth without it," the girl replied. "Really wide."

"May I see?" The girl nodded and Paddy took the flash off.

They rode around and sure enough the mare began to open her mouth. He pursed his lips a little.

"Ok, I see the problem." He called her over.

"Right, now, let's start here," he held her hands a little.

"As you're riding around, your hands are flapping, like a birds wing," he chuckled and she smirked.

"Up and down, up and down, it's like they're doing rising trot," she smiled again.

"Now, that's not so nice for your pony's mouth, is it?"

A thoughtful frown crossed the girls face and she nodded.

"So, let's try when you trot to keep these very steady. Now, we don't want statue hands," the smirk was back.

"No concrete grasps, we want give and take forwards and backwards, but we want steady." He turned to the whole ride.

"Things that make horses mouths gape include dental issues like hooks and sharp teeth, mouth damage, bit problems, tension, and the rider's hands.

Flashes don't solve any of these problems. What solves the problem of horses mouth's opening is finding the reason why and putting it right." He looked at the girl.

"Don't be ashamed of flappy hands, be ashamed of having flappy hands and not addressing the problem."

She beamed at him. "I'll try."

"Good girl, let's have a look." The girl proceeded to walk around keeping her hands much more quiet and the mare flicked her ears and didn't open her mouth at all.

"Look at that," Paddy smiled. "Let's see a trot."

Even I could tell from my stable that the little girl was trying hard to do as she was told, and it paid off. Sure, her hands weren't completely steady, and sure the mare gaped a little, but there was a massive improvement in both.

"That's so much better." Paddy smiled.

"Can you tell mummy?" the girl asked. "So she knows what I have to do?"

"That I will young lady," Paddy grinned.

Just like that he'd set a young rider on a new path. A better one. I thought of Emma, I bet she would love Paddy. He was what she aspired to be.

The bevy of girls with Irish Draughts came in next. One look at Paddy's face and I knew he saw what I did. He frowned.

"What's with all these matching saddles?" He asked.

"Aren't they amazing!" One girl enthused. "They're RVTT saddles and are very expensive. But Claus Klein the top German eventer is amazing and he uses them on all his horses! We only want the best for our horses."

Paddy shook his head. "Young lady, the best saddle is what fits your horse, and I can tell you now this lot don't." He shook his head.

"Look here, you trot round, the rest can watch. Look at the tension in the horse, the stiff hindquarters. A saddle isn't a car. Just because it's endorsed by a top international rider doesn't mean it's the best for your horse."

He inspected one of the saddles. "Look, this would sit fine on something warmblood shaped probably, but even with a few alterations it will never fit your boy here properly, and it's stopping him from moving freely."

He carried on with his lesson, but frequently pointed out where things were stiff or could be better and refused to do any jumping with them.

Afterwards I heard a couple of the girls moaning about him. They went on about how much they had paid for the saddles and how there was no way they'd change them because of some old-time eventer. A couple of the other girls were already calling their saddle fitter. I knew whose horse I'd rather be. I felt sorry for the horses of those girls who thought more about how much they had spent than if their horses were comfortable.

The last lesson of the day was Murphy. He and Bridget had a 1-1 class. She came in looking a little flustered and apologised for being a little late. They started work and Paddy seemed very pleased with how she rode. He gave her pointers and was genuinely happy by her responses, but also by the questions she asked.

"He's a nice fella you got," he said at the end of their class.

Bridget sighed. "He is. I wish we could keep competing."

"You can't?" Paddy asked.

She shook her head. "The vet confirmed he has mild arthritis starting. I can't afford two horses, so this is my last season. Well, unless I can find a cheaper yard to go to. That's what I'm looking for, but everywhere I've seen that I could afford two horses, has no school or facilities."

Paddy nodded at her a little. "You'd be a good fit at mine I think, yes. Look, I'm looking for a new stable hand. One of my regular staff has gone and got themselves a place on the national event team and my weekend girl is taking her place. How would you like to work for me on the weekends and some school holidays? Pay is decent and I'll give you half price on livery, that way two horses cost the same as one."

Bridget's mouth fell open and a second later she began to cry.

"Oh, yes, yes please." She flopped down on Murphy's neck and hugged him.

"Ah here, get on with you," Paddy laughed. "You'll be getting his mane all damp."

Bridget smiled through her tears and I stood watching feeling very happy for her and Murphy. She had put him first and the universe seemed to be thanking her for it on Murphy's behalf. Not for the first time I wished Siobhan was more like Bridget.

Chapter 37

Not long after Murphy and Bridget left to work, and in Murphy's case, live at Paddy's, I found myself facing my biggest eventing competition yet. I'd fully recovered from my tying up and true to her word, Siobhan had changed my routine. My feed was different, my warm ups and cool downs longer, and I was out in the field more too. We'd competed again and so far I'd had no problems. To make things a little better for me, Siobhan had started paying Laura to come with us to events, to help warm me up and keep an eye on me. She travelled with us to one event before she suggested I go on the horsebox in company, and so from then on when I went somewhere, I travelled with another horse, either from our stables, or from one close by going to the same event.

One of the horses who frequently joined me was Missy. She was a large Irish Draught/Thoroughbred cross with an elegant head and a kindly manner. She doted on her human, a slightly older man with dark hair called Fin. He always came across as standoffish, but once alone with Missy, he'd revert to patting her and chatting to her in a much more open way. It made me smile.

Missy always seemed as laid back as her rider. That was until one morning towards the end of the summer. The heatwave had subsided, but it was still mild. Missy trotted onto the horsebox excitedly. She was a mare who loved to jump, genuinely, soaring over fences made her happy, and today she was ecstatic. Laura was helping Fin load in a lot of things we didn't usually take with us to an event and I was surprised.

"What's happening?" I asked Missy.

"Don't you know?" she replied, her eyes glinting. "This is the big event. The three-day event. We go and stay over at the course, it's huge. Dressage is on day one, cross country is on day two and show jumping is on day three."

She rattled on about the event, but I lost track of her words. I'd never done a three-day event before. It sounded a little scary. I felt a knot form in my stomach that didn't go away even that evening when we arrived at our temporary accommodation. I was glad Laura was there, she spent ages making sure I was settled in my stable, checking me and keeping me calm.

The first day of the competition wasn't so bad. We did dressage as Missy said we would. I tried hard to please Siobhan, moving as flowingly as I could. Apparently, I did well. Siobhan was pleased, and Laura made a big fuss of me, and took me off on a lead rope for some grass in hand so I wasn't stuck in my stable.

It was while I was doing this I got my first glimpse of the cross country course. I normally liked cross-country. I liked the rustic fences and the cantering between them through countryside. These fences though were huge. To Missy, who was a clear hand and a half bigger than I was, I'm sure they looked fine, but to me they were terrifying. This, I decided, was above my grade.

The worried feeling I got looking at those jumps didn't fade as Siobhan prepared us for our round. I remember lining up ready to go and not wanting to do it. A buzzer sounded and Siobhan set us off. I couldn't refuse. I just had to do my best and hope it was good enough to get us round.

Fence after fence came at us, each one as big and taxing as the last. I started to worry about getting my feet in the right places, muddled by the different sights, heights and bends. At one point I stumbled a little, my legs starting to tire. I felt sore afterwards but tried not to think about the pain, just concentrating on where we were going and the next fence to scramble over.

A strange panicked feeling came over me, as if I had tunnel vision and could see only the fences and nothing else. My lungs felt sore again, my breath more ragged than it had been for years. I couldn't focus, my leg hurt and my chest burnt. I tried to slow but Siobhan pushed me on.

We turned through a little patch of trees and then, up ahead came a log followed by a huge V shaped fence. I'd seen these before. The easiest way was to jump the log and the two smaller legs of the V, but I knew Siobhan would go for the huge, tight point of the V. I knew she'd pull me that way. I knew my sore leg would take the brunt of the turn, and I knew there was nothing I could do to stop what was coming. I could try to pull towards the smaller fence, but she wouldn't let me.

I made the log and sure enough she pulled me sharply at the point of the V. I tried to make the turn, but my leg gave out. I felt myself tumbling over, my whole body hitting the ground with a thump. I lost track of Siobhan, unsure where she had landed, knowing only she wasn't in the saddle. I came to a stop by the fence and lay on the ground for a second not sure what exactly had just happened to me. There was silence all around.

Suddenly Laura was there catching my reins. She looked terrified, worried, her face pale. "Please get up," she begged me in a whisper. "Please be able to get up."

I looked at her, and with a huge effort stood upright. She started to cry. I limped away from the fence stiffly following her. I looked around. Siobhan was lying next to the fence clutching her leg and crying. There were people there in high-vis vests talking to her. I heard someone on the radio call for a paramedic.

"She'll be ok," Laura said to me. "Let's take care of you." I realised I didn't much care that Siobhan was injured. I followed Laura without looking back.

The vet who examined me at the event was very thorough. Laura stayed with me to hear her verdict. I had done something to my stifle.

"His jumping days are done," the vet concluded eventually. "I mean, he'll pop a cross pole maybe, little things, but..."

"Look, I saw that fall, it was nasty, but it was not his fault. I think he was lame before the take off," Laura pulled out her phone and showed the vet something. The woman nodded her head.

Laura took me home the next morning. Once again, I was on box rest. She would leave the radio on for me to listen to and come check on me during the day. She told me Siobhan was angry, I presumed at me. She had broken her leg, but would be alright. She told me not to worry though. She'd posted the footage of our fall on line anonymously along with a comment about me being slightly lame before the jump. Blame was put squarely on my being injured before the fall, so Siobhan couldn't say much.

I wondered if Emma had seen the footage. I hoped she hadn't. It would make her worry about me even more. I missed her. I began to wonder what would happen next. I knew Siobhan wouldn't keep me. I couldn't jump and in her mind, I was the reason she had been injured. I was moving on, and I knew it.

Chapter 38

Siobhan didn't even show up to say goodbye the day I moved. It was left up to Laura to pack up my things and make sure I was safely loaded up with my new owner. It proved once and for all to me that Siobhan had only ever seen me as a thing. A tool used to compete and nothing more. The thought should have saddened me, but it surprisingly didn't. I'd already known what she was like. This was just one more example of it. I wondered if being sold on might not be a good thing. Part of me worried I'd end up somewhere bad, or with a human who cared as little for me as Siobhan did, but given her comments about Murphy, I guessed it could have been worse. I was alive and there was a chance I'd fall on my feet. I prayed that was the case.

When the horsebox turned up for me and Laura came to put my headcollar on, I nuzzled into her hoping she knew it meant I appreciated how much she had done for me while I was in her care. I think she did. She looked a little misty eyed as she handed me over to my new human, and I heard her tell the lady who had bought me to take care of me. I looked over at her, Laura, not an owner, but certainly the human who had cared for me most while I was here, as I stepped onto the ramp. I was 14 years old and I had no idea what my future would be.

An older man with a flat cap put a hand on my rump and gave me a little push of encouragement. "Up you go lad."

I did as asked and stepped up onto the horsebox. The man smiled at me as my new owner tied me up before slipping out and helping him close the back of the horsebox up. I realised from their conversation that he had been hired to transport me. I flicked my ears and listened more intently, hoping to learn something about who had bought me and where I was going.

My new owner was in her early thirties, smart and kindly. Her name was Aoife and I was her first horse, so she said, but she'd been around horses for years. I tried to feel optimistic about my new home. At least she told the driver she didn't compete, well not yet, and probably not beyond a few local shows. I liked the sound of that. A happy hacker, that's what she called herself. Someone who liked to potter around the countryside on a horse, maybe a few little canters here and there, but mostly gentle rides.

My mind flicked back to the days with Emma when we'd wander down the track with Wizzy. Would that be my life again? Aoife wasn't Emma, but the life she described sounded nice. I started to hope this was it. I'd find a caring forever home with gentle trail rides and a nice human. How I hoped that was true. Maybe I wouldn't be with Emma, but I could be safe and content. As a horse there was a lot to be said for that.

We travelled to a place called Thurles, in Co. Tipperary. It seemed nice, at least the part I saw. My new home was a small yard with lush looking, rolling green fields. There were a couple of herds of up to five horses, each one with two large fields, one for the summer and one for winter. I was introduced to Lucky and Star who would become my new field mates after a few days. I liked Lucky instantly. He reminded me very much of Dougal, although he was much taller than the Shetland. He was jolly and inquisitive, coming over to me as soon as I was turned out to say hello.

Within an hour I think I'd heard Lucky's entire life story. He said he was a kids pony, passed around from one child to the next, but always staying within the same area and always sold on through human family networks to someone he knew. It was the way life was, he said. Little humans outgrow little ponies, so they move on, but being good at teaching children how to ride, meant he was never short of a willing home. He seemed proud of that. I wondered what happened when he was too old to teach children. Was he a tool too? Did he know either way?

Star, by contrast, was a quiet, tall leggy bay thoroughbred with a large white star on his forehead and long white stockings up his legs. He'd been a race horse I learnt, but only for a short time.

Like several of my earliest friends he'd been started under saddle much too early. He certainly hadn't been started slowly. By the age of two he was on the track, running and running while a human jockey whipped at his hind quarters to go ever faster. The thought gave me nightmares. He'd fallen eventually, stumbling over his own feet as he desperately tried to go quicker. Memories of my own accident with Siobhan flooded back. At least, I thought, when I fell it was alone, not surrounded by other stampeding hooves. Star had been injured in his fall too. Like me, his career was over.

In a way Star was one of the luckiest horses I met in my life. He came from a place where he had value only if he won. Fell, injured and worthless he could easily have been sent for meat, or sold to someone cheaply who cared nothing for him. That was how it was for many of those failed racehorses, especially the gelded ones.

Star though had been bought by a lady called Lisa who rehabilitated ex-racehorses. She made it her life's mission to take on those dumped, broken and often fearful horses from the track and train them to be useful riding horses. Star had been taken on as a project to sell, but something about him had touched her heart and now he was Lisa's forever horse. She still took on other ex-racers, trained them, worked with them, and teaching them how to behave off the track, before finding them new and loving homes, but Star was a permanent fixture.

I liked Lisa. She knew a lot of things and told Aoife how to do things in ways that would help me. Her advice always seemed to come from a place of kindness and always from a horse's perspective. I had landed on my feet, I thought one morning as I looked out over the dewy fields watching the sun rise to greet the day.

Chapter 39

Aoife came to see me pretty regularly, but most of the time she visited only once a day to simply check me over, pick out my feet and otherwise she left me be. Usually, Lisa checked me in the evening too, a second glance to make sure I still had four feet and two ears. It wasn't the worst situation I had been in, but as the days rolled by, I decided it wasn't the best either.

While I had been with Siobhan I longed to be outside more, in the fields with my friends. Now I had just that, but I started missing the attention. I'd been spoilt by Emma I realised. I had been fussed over, loved, hacked, and spent time with both my human and my friends. Now when one or the other was missing from my life, I felt somehow lost and hollow. Star and Lucky were regularly taken out for longer hacks or lessons and I'd find myself alone in the field. I didn't like that much. Since I always knew they'd come back so I tried to make the best of things, but it was a reminder of how much more time they spent with their humans than I did with mine.

Aoife did come and brush me and take me out on little rides, but they were shorter than the ones I was used too. I felt squeezed in, as if she were always hurrying through our exercise because she had somewhere else to be, something else to do. The only time she really spent any quality time with me was on a Saturday. It quickly became a highlight I'd look forward to, a part of my week that was more exciting and interesting than the rest.

I'd come in and have some chaff and carrots early on Saturdays. Aoife would then groom me until my coat was free of dirt and mud. She would detangle my mane and tail and in general make me look smart. After that she'd have a cup of tea and chat with a few other liveries until I had fully digested breakfast. Then she would tack me up and off we'd go for a longer walk.

I missed my bitless bridle on these longer rides, but thanks to Lisa's advice, I had been fitted with a loose ring snaffle. It wasn't perfect as it pinched the corners of my lips sometimes, but Aoife had light hands, so there was no bruising inside my mouth. I saw the vet, farrier, and equine dentist regularly with her.

Yes, in all life was tolerable, if not perfect. I didn't want for food, I knew if I needed something it would be provided, but I didn't feel like I was Aoife's world, not like I had with Emma. Perhaps, I thought, that was because Aoife was a grown up, that all humans turned out that way as they grew, that somehow the magic feeling between me and Emma had something to do with her youth. I hoped I was wrong, that adult Emma would be the same as teen Emma, but when I looked at Aoife, doubt crept into my mind.

We usually always went on the same trail ride. It was loop around several fields opposite the little yard, on week days we only did the first two fields, but on the weekends that doubled to four fields and we'd do two loops.

The trail was easy, and safe, but it became dull quickly. At first, I thought it was because this was the only route we had so I tried to shake off my boredom, but I saw Star and Lucky heading in different directions, so I knew that wasn't it.

Perhaps, I thought, Aoife was nervous, that was why she took the same, safe, known route. She did sit stiffly in the saddle, I mused as we trudged around one morning. I decided that must be it. I was Aoife's first horse and she was worried. The best thing to do, I thought, was to be careful with her. I only went faster when she asked me to. I tried not to spook, and I was always ready to step sideways when opening and closing the gate. I hoped that the more she saw I was calm and well behaved, the more she would trust me, and eventually we could do some more interesting rides.

After a few months it finally happened. Lisa persuaded Aoife to take me out on a longer ride with her and Star. I was so excited. The joy of being anywhere but the loop made me almost giddy. I jogged a little as we headed away from the yard and felt Aoife tense even more than usual. I had to calm down. I had to if I stood any chance of this being more than a one off.

Thankfully Lisa was there to help keep Aoife calm too and tell her it was alright. I wasn't being bad; I was just excited. We began to settle into a steady ride together, me trying to keep pace with Star's longer stride without jogging and upsetting Aoife. We went up through a little thicket and came out at a long wide-open field. It reminded me of the cross-country fields and again I could sense Aoife's nerves as soon as we stepped into the wide expanse. I felt suddenly sad. For some reason she expected me to do something wrong, to bolt or buck maybe. I hated that she thought I could do that to her. Worse, I looked at the field longing to canter through the lush grass, to feel the wind in my mane, freedom. I wanted to run, but I couldn't.

I pictured myself standing there with Emma. She would have looked over the long trail with the gentle upward slope and I know she would have let us go, let us run together, be free and wild. Emma. I missed her still so much. I knew with Aoife there would be no race across the grass, no freedom. I'd be walking. I'd have to so she knew she could trust me.

True enough we walked the field. I plodded along losing my momentum and enthusiasm with every step. So, this was my life now. Slow, steady and dull. Perhaps there was a chance Aoife would change, become more confident with me over time, but I didn't bet on it.

Humans, I had learned, were creatures of habit. I feared this was it. I prepared for a life that was safe but boring. It wasn't so bad, I told myself over and over. I was safe and I had my needs met. But every time I told myself that, a little part of me cried out for the life I'd had with Emma.

Chapter 40

My life with Aoife trundled on in a mundane, stable manner for the rest of the year, and then I noticed she began to visit less. At first it was just our Saturday rides reducing to two fields, and since the weather was turning, I didn't mind so much. Then, over the next few weeks, as it grew colder and wetter, she appeared less and less and for shorter and shorter periods. I was confused. Had I done something wrong? I looked back over our rides, searching my memory for some incident that might have caused her detachment, but I found none.

I started to notice how cold it was getting. I usually had a lovely thick coat and plenty of food to keep me toasty, with the addition of a rug when it turned very bitter, or the rain was consistent and heavy.

This year though, I had a trace clip and Aoife was not around much. I was often cold, wet, and hungry. She'd feed me when she turned up, and if it was a wet day might throw a rug on me, but more often than not that made things worse. The rug would get saturated and left on me, making me feel damp and itchy.

Lisa would often slip me food. She'd tut to herself and moan about Aoife saying she should loan me out, or pay someone to come take care of me if she couldn't do it herself. It seemed to irritate her that she couldn't do something about me. She'd often say things like 'I'd take that wet rug off if I could'. I didn't understand why she couldn't. She could see I was miserable and cold. Lucky said it's because I wasn't hers, and if she did that she could get in trouble.

I could feel myself becoming thinner. My energy levels dropping, especially as it got colder and colder. My legs felt tired. I longed for a dry warm stable to curl up in and sleep for just a couple of hours. I dreamed of warm feeds, buckets of oats and carrots. I was 15 years old now but felt like I was 30.

I thought back to the winter with Emma, the rugs changed with the temperature drops, taken off and changed if they were wet through. Good food. An advent calendar. They all seemed like far away distant figments of imagination compared to my current situation.

By December I was wondering if Wizzy had his Christmas stocking. His 'mum' would have bundled him in thick rugs so he looked like a walking blanket. I'd been amused at the sight of him all kitted out, but he felt the cold and would shiver if he wasn't bundled up, a legacy, he said, of descending from horses born in hot climates. As I stood cold and shivering in the frozen field it suddenly didn't seem amusing anymore.

Frost formed on my whiskers and the tips of my mane. Then the snow began to fall. It covered the last of the green grass in my field. Now I had to dig for it, or lay down in the cold snowy ground to melt the white stuff. Neither was pleasant. Lucky and Star were brought in and fed twice a day.

Sometimes I'd wander over to the gate hoping their humans would feed me too, or that Aoife would turn up. Neither happened. Lisa would scoop up hay though, and toss it over the gate so I had something. She'd rub my face, pity evident in her voice when she'd say 'You deserve better little man'. Did I? I was starting to wonder. I was starting to feel like I had done something bad, something to deserve this. Lisa's words reminded me I hadn't. I was just stuck at the whim of a human, and yet another one who didn't seem to put my needs or wants as a high priority.

That winter was the longest of my life. It was hard and cold. A bitter, biting cold I'd never experienced the like of before. I knew I was slowly, steadily losing condition. I could feel my little thin rug become looser on my neck and middle. When I drank from the trough, I hardly recognised the face reflected back at me. My neck, the part I could see of it anyway, was hollow, visibly, even with my thicker winter coat at the top of my neck. My mane and tail became a knotted, tangled mess. When I swished my tail about, I could feel it was clumpy, not smooth, and silky as it had been. It was now covered in heavy, hardened clumps of mud. I was itchy too. Under the rug. I wanted it off, but I knew if I did tear it apart to scratch, I'd be all the colder.

I must have started to look very bad by the time the first signs of spring came around. I know this because Lisa called the yard owner on the phone while she was standing next to the paddock. The yard was owned by an old farmer I'd only seen a few times the summer before when he'd come by to fix a fence.

"Honestly Cormac, he's in a right state, if she doesn't start coming back down I'm calling the welfare people, he's that bad. Someone needs to call her and get her down here. I'm not paying to hay her horse another week, and he needs feed. Proper feed. It's heart-breaking, and I've texted her and told her he's in a bad way, and she's still not come up. I figure if you tell her... thanks Cormac."

She hung up and glanced in my direction with a sad smile.

Aoife did come the next day and with her was a baby. I suddenly understood. I hadn't been neglected, I hadn't been abandoned, I'd got a brother! I was suddenly happy. I had a small person to love, and one who would love me, I knew he would. He would grow up and be like Chloe and I would show him the wonders of horses.

I was so happy even in my weakened state I managed to trot over to the fence. I pushed my nose over the fence to sniff the little pink fingers that stuck out of the pale blue baby suit. Aoife let out a little squeal and pulled the baby away, flicking my nose with her other hand. I pulled my head back sharply. It didn't really hurt, not physically, but I felt as if I'd had an electric shock. I stood staring at her and the baby. I didn't have a small person to love. I didn't have a human. I'd been rejected, and I knew it.

"He's only trying to say hello," Lisa huffed. "Given the state you let him get in if I were you I'd be happy he came over to me at all."

"I've been busy with the baby," Aoife retorted.

"Well, if you're that busy with the baby," Lisa replied a little sharply, "I'd pass him on to someone who actually cares, because we will not cover for you anymore. Look at him! He's half the horse he was. You might not like to hear it, but you're negligent. If the welfare lot saw him you wouldn't need to pass him on because they'd cart him off in a second."

Aoife looked at the seething Lisa, her lip quivering a little, but it had little effect on Star's human. "I tell you what, why don't you leave him with me. I'll feed him, get some weight on him, and find him someone who'll give him a decent home. You can just pay the bills. It's what you should have done when you first started having trouble getting down and I offered to help."

Aoife sighed. "Fine."

It was the last word I heard her say. She turned and headed back to her car without a second glance in my direction. I was looking for a new home. Again.

Chapter 41

Lisa did exactly what she said she would. I was suddenly being taken care of again, but I knew the goal of it was to sell me on. I appreciated the food, the changed rugs and the brushing, but I didn't feel happy. Once again, I was going to move on. It was a matter of when, not if. Under Lisa's care I put on a little weight, though I was still thin and most of my muscles had wasted away. Still, as the weather began to improve a steady stream of people began to appear to see me.

A lot of those who came by commented on my apparent 'state'. I learnt from Lisa's conversations with these people that I was being sold cheaply because of my condition and injury. I was worth less than I had been. I couldn't quite get my mind around that. I was worth less to humans because another human had neglected to feed me. I was worth less to humans because another human had made me jump a fence and I fell. I was worth less. How did humans put prices on my life? Were they worth less if they were hurt? Worth less if they were left hungry? Why should my value be in what I could do for them, for how well I could jump or perform? Did my existence not have a value? Did the fact I could safely take a rider out for a hack mean I was worth less than if I could jump a cross country fence? It hurt my mind thinking about that.

I was relieved some of the people who came didn't buy me. Some of them wanted to ride me while I wasn't certain I had the strength to carry them. One girl though, she looked at me kindly. Her mother was talking to Lisa, asking lots of questions about me and my past.

"She'll do dressage, and of course I lined up the best, THE best, trainer in Kildare for her," the mother rambled on. "He can do dressage, can't he?"

"He has a lovely movement," Lisa assured her. "When he's fit."

"He looks sad," the girl said. She brushed my forelock from my face a little and smiled at me. "Would you like to come home with us?"

I decided I thought I would. Of all the people who had ever owned me, young girls had so far proven the nicest. I wasn't so sure about the girl's mother. She seemed a little boastful and blustery, but I looked at the girl who could tell I was sad and was reassured.

"I'm not sure," the mother looked at me sceptically. "He's a lot of money Hannah, if he can't do what you want him too."

"You mean what you want him to do, what you want me to do," Hannah huffed. "I just want to ride and he seems so sweet. I want a horse I can trust, not one who moves prettily."

"Trustworthy I assure you he is," Lisa smiled over at me. "Even in prime condition. You'll want that for your daughter of course."

"Oh, yes, yes, of course. I mean safety first, of course," the mother muttered.

With that I knew Hannah and Lisa had won her round. I had another new human. I had high hopes of Hannah, she seemed to see me as a living breathing being, not an object. My mind flicked back to Emma, thinking about the time we had spent together. I wondered, no, I hoped, Hannah would be like Emma, only an Emma who would own me and keep me forever.

Life with Hannah and her mother, Deirdre, started off well on the whole. I moved to Kildare, to a medium sized stable yard. It had several stables, a few large fields, and a little outdoor school with a nice, firm sandy surface. I spent quite some time doing very little. Hannah insisted she would not ride, or work me in any way, until I had gained some weight back. Only then would we begin to, as she put it, 'build me up'.

I was stabled overnight, but every day I was turned out for a good length of time. The grass was green and lush, I was given hay and feed. Slowly I began to return to my former glory. Hannah brushed me daily until my coat began to look silky and smooth again. The remaining tangles in my mane and tail were carefully combed through with a brush and an awful lot of sweet smelling detangler fluid. No matter what happened in my future life, I will always appreciate the time Hannah took with me. She put me right before we started any work. She did that out of kindness and I was determined to repay her for it.

Deirdre on the other hand was loud. Very, very loud. I'd never met a human quite like her before. She didn't seem to ride, although she was constantly talking about what she had done in her youth.

She'd competed, she'd won, ridden at this ride or that ride, been to shows. The list seemed endless. Her past glories always seemed better than those of the humans she was talking to. I noticed she did this with me too. It was often reported that I was a 'pure' bred Connemara, and that I had done big events in my past. My fall and injury were not so well publicised. She was also the one who changed my name.

"Lir," she frowned when I had first been unloaded. "Not a very horsey name, is it Hannah? How about we call him Storm. That's a proper horse name and its part of his official name on his passport."

Hannah had given her a withering look but didn't argue. So for the first time in my life I was given a new name.

When her mother would drone on and on about these things, Hannah would shake her head and usually put the radio on, I think in a vague way to drown out the sound of her mother. One thing was true though, she had lined up a professional trainer to work with Hannah and I when I was fully fit again. I hoped it was someone like Paddy. A professional trainer, I thought, who would help us. Someone who understood horses that could ensure I was ridden well, and, most importantly, kindly.

As I grew stronger, I became more and more interested in the trainer. In what I could learn to do. I was keen to show Hannah how well I could do some dressage moves I knew already, shoulder in, or turn on the forehand. I could do those. A new world of possibilities began to emerge as my energy levels returned. I had a home, food, care, and someone who seemed keen to go out and do things too. No more boring hacks around the same field, I was going to get the best of both worlds, and maybe, just maybe, this time, I'd found my forever home.

A forever home. I still wished it was with Emma, but I was starting to see that wishes don't come true. I had to move on, even if I didn't really want to. I had to hold my good past memories close, cherish them, but also to look forward, live with what I had and hope that when I found a good place I could stay there until I was old.

Humans, some humans, did that. They took care of horses when they were too old to do work anymore, would just love them, and care for them as part of their family. Some horses were lucky, not tossed aside but honoured by their humans for the work they had done in the past. That was what I really needed, what I wanted. I wanted a safe forever home with no more moving, no more being sold on. A stable home where I was happy and loved.

Chapter 42

I settled in nicely to my new home with Hannah. I had several field mates, but found myself drawn to two in particular. We made an odd trio. Rory was a 15.2hh cob with thick feathery feet and a happy laid-back attitude, while Meave was a pretty little full Arab mare who stood at only 14hh. No one seemed to understand why we three gravitated towards each other, but we did, mostly out of shared experiences. Both Rory and Meave had been, as Rory put it, around the block a few times and each of us were now hoping we had found our forever homes.

Rory had been with his human for three years now and was beginning to feel much more confident about his future. He said it made a huge difference when you felt secure in your human, that you didn't wake up scared this was the day things would change. I understood that. I hoped one day I would feel like he did, certain in my life. Meave was less confident even though she had been with her human a little longer. She wouldn't say exactly why, but I could tell her past hadn't been a good one.

I hadn't been there long when a fourth horse joined our trio. His name was Major. He was a huge grey Irish Draught cross that had once been an event horse, but had retired to a life of occasional sedate hacking. I stood in awe of Major's life story. It was what I think every horse dreams of.

His owner had brought him on slowly as a youngster. He had been first ridden as a four year old. He was kindly trained, ridden in well fitted tack and always cared for carefully. His human had competed him at a high level, but had been careful that any hint of pain was investigated thoroughly. Now, as he was too old and stiff to keep doing his job, he had come here to relax. No, he had not been sold. His human hadn't palmed him off as a loan horse as Alison had with me. No, Major's human was still there daily to check and tend to him. Groom him, love him, and in fine weather when he felt able, to go for walks and hacks.

Several years before, she had bought a youngster, Bobby Socks, who was brought on, just as slowly, to replace Major in all event activities. He arrived a few weeks after Major and settled in to our herd, favouring playing with the younger horses rather than grazing quietly with us. I wondered what it would be like to have had only one human for my whole life. One who cared for me so much, that when the time came I would be retired and a new, lucky horse would be added to our family. I thought about Bridget and Murphy. That was what she had planned to do, and I thought of Siobhan suggesting a horse be put down when they were of no further use. How different, I thought, humans could be.

My own humans were proving interesting. Hannah was lovely. She slowly began to work me, not in-hand as I had hoped, but on long-lines so at least there was no lunging. Soon enough I found myself being fitted for a saddle too. Once that was sorted, we were off. Hannah liked to hack and I loved it. We went anywhere and everywhere. I had missed going out and seeing things, a sense of freedom crept into my world again.

There were woods to walk through on warm days with cool little streams to splash my legs with chilly water. Banks to canter up, trails to follow, and even, after checking with a vet it was alright to do so, a few, very small logs to hop over. Hannah was always careful when we jumped a log. Too big and I'd feel my stifle twinge, but small ones, those I could still happily jump over and enjoy!

We went back to the beach again too, often with Rory and his human, since she was only a little older than Hannah. I loved the beach. I loved the sand and cantering along the shore by the waves. It made me happy, and a little sad as memories of past rides flooded back.

I still missed Emma, but I was learning to trust Hannah, and one day, I thought, maybe I'd love her as much. After all, Hannah was kind, she had gentle hands, took me on nice rides, paid attention to me and looked after me well. Why shouldn't I love her?

I thought about what Rory had said, about starting to feel safe and secure in his life. I wondered if when I started to feel like that, I'd also love Hannah as I had Emma. One day, I mused, I will wake up and feel 100% safe in my life. I will realise I am in a forever home and I will love my human, not just want to take care of them for loyalty's sake, but love them.

Yet, as the days ticked by something niggled at me. For all the care, for all the attention, kindness and good treatment, something bothered me. Emma would always talk about us as this team, what we could do in the future, how I'd help her be this wonderful teacher of humans. I was in her dreams. With Hannah though, she didn't mention me in her future, her dreams. I told myself that was because I couldn't help Hannah achieve her dreams. She wanted to do something called architecture and I was pretty sure horses didn't do that. Still, it bothered me, just a little.

Hannah's mother also worried me. She wanted us to compete. Hannah didn't really like competitions. They weren't, as she put it, her 'thing'. She liked open spaces, lovely pretty, natural views and wandering along daydreaming, having the odd canter, and basically enjoying life.

Deirdre however wanted to prove we were the best. She seemed to think without ribbons or trophies there was no proof Hannah could ride. I was confused by that, it was clear Hannah could ride, we galloped along beaches, we navigated steep slopes in trees, was that not proof enough? I realised though; it was more about bragging rights. Deirdre wanted ribbons and rosettes so she could brag. She wanted Hannah to compete so she could go around saying 'oh, my daughter did this' or 'my daughter won that', just as she did with her own past glories.

Not a week went by when Deirdre didn't suggest we do some competition or other. The closest we got though were a few long-distance rides that Hannah liked the sound of. I was happy with that. I'd done competitions before. I knew that they didn't prove you were a good rider, or a good owner. They could be fun, if you went out only to enjoy yourself, but if

Siobhan had taught me nothing else it was that competitions were not the best measure of a human, or a horse. What type of team you made in an emergency was more important than what you looked like in a show ring. I had proven that too all those years ago with John and Chloe.

Chapter 43

I got away with hacking about with Hannah until one unfortunate morning when it was a little icy and she took me into the little outdoor school instead of out around the fields. It was a busy morning and a few others joined us in the arena. It was the first time most of them had seen me work. Hannah had us walk, trot and canter around warming up, and then practise a few dressage moves she knew helped us out hacking. Moving my hind quarters, stepping sideways when asked, all the things that helped us on our wanderings.

"He's got a lovely movement," one of the older ladies in the school commented.

"Thanks," Hannah replied to the compliment. I felt proud too, it was nice to be told I moved nicely. Unfortunately for me the lady's compliment had a much farther reaching effect.

Apparently, later that morning, she passed the same comment on to Deirdre. She came bustling over to my stable with a huge smile on her face.

"Mrs. Cairn just said she saw you riding today and Storm moved beautifully. We should make more of him Hannah. Why don't I give Cillian O'Dowd a ring, you know he's a professional, and you did promise to take lessons when Storm was fit again."

Hannah grumped. "Yeah, but, I meant lessons from Mrs. Murphy from Oakwood, she teaches all my friends, and she's super nice."

Deirdre sighed. "I'm offering a professional Hannah, someone a lot better than Mrs. Murphy," she rolled her eyes.

"Fine, fine," she continued. "I'll take him to lessons with Cillian. He needs to do something so his potential isn't wasted. If you like you can sort something out with Mrs. Murphy here when the weather improves a bit."

Hannah smiled, but I felt confused and alarmed. I didn't want Deirdre to ride me. I wasn't sure I much liked her. I liked Hannah. Hannah was my human, not her mum, wasn't she? Or was I to be shared? I wasn't sure I liked that idea. It also worried me that Deirdre talked about me being wasted. I wasn't being wasted. I was enjoying my life, and I was pretty sure Hannah was too. I didn't feel like I was being wasted by not competing or doing high end lessons. From the sound of things, I started to think I'd much rather have lessons here on the yard with Hannah and Mrs. Murphy too, rather than going off somewhere to work with some professional trainer and Deirdre.

My misgivings proved all too true. One morning Deirdre turned up with a friend and loaded me onto a little horsebox she had borrowed for the day. We didn't go far, thankfully, and when I was unloaded, I found myself at a large, very tidy, equestrian centre.

Every gadget going seemed to be there. Big metal horse walkers with a couple of bored looking horses, circling around and around in them. A huge arena, and as I peered inside a large shed, I caught sight of a stable with heat lamps above it, and a horse standing drying beneath them.

"Look at this," Deirdre shook her head a huge smile on her face. "And to think Hannah wouldn't take advantage of this. I mean, it's so posh and fancy."

"They have everything here," her friend agreed.

I looked at the numb, bored looking faces of the horses around me. They have everything here, I thought, except for happy horses. The pristine fields were empty and I soon realised all the horses were inside, stabled, rugged and alone. I looked at the green grass wondering why they were inside. As if in answer to my question Deirdre's friend piped up with an answer.

"Look, they even keep the horses in when the ground is wet so the fields look nice and the gateways don't get muddy." She sounded as if she were in awe of this, as if having a pretty field and a clean gateway made the yard better. I thought the fields looked bare and unnatural. Lucy had always put something down around the gate if it got too wet, and put up a little electric fence around the muddy part so we didn't 'wallow like hippos' she said. Apparently, that wasn't good enough for this place though.

I was tacked up and taken into the big arena. This was the place I first met the professional trainer Cillian O'Dowd. I use the term professional very loosely, for a professional with horses I am certain he was not.

He began by having Deirdre get on and ride me around so he could 'see what he was dealing with'. Deirdre sat more heavily than Hannah, and her hands were harder on my mouth. I felt uncomfortable with her and struggled to adjust to her newness.

Cillian O'Dowd didn't seem to notice my discomfort, nor did he take into account that we had never actually ridden together before. He began yelling out instructions to Deirdre.

"More leg, much more, leg, leg, leg, get him moving, he needs to be more forward. Don't let him back off that leg."

Deirdre booted me on a little. I was used to light taps from Hannah, not so with Deirdre. Whenever O'Dowd said leg, she kicked. My ribs began to hurt.

"More contact, he's poking his nose out, he needs to tuck that chin in." Deirdre pulled on the reins more. Not a gentle pressure, but an almost constant tugging.

"Better," O'Dowd yelled. Better for who I thought. "Still not forward enough. Come in."

Deirdre pulled me up in the centre of the arena. She seemed out of breath. "Oh, I think I need to get a bit fitter," she almost giggled. O'Dowd smiled; it didn't look pleasant to me.

"Pop off, I'll see if I can get him going."

Deirdre slid off and O'Dowd hopped on me. As he jumped up, I noticed a gleam to his boots. If the glint hadn't been enough to tell me he was wearing spurs, his next action would have left me with no uncertainty. He booted me. The sharp metal prongs dug into my sides and I sprang away from the sensation.

"That's got him going," O'Dowd chuckled. "You need a pair of these. Gerr on with ya," he yelled at me.

For the next ten minutes he jabbed at my sides, pulled at my mouth, and asked me to almost contort my body into a pose that was so alien it hurt in places I barely knew existed. When it was over, he had Deirdre get back on and proceeded to 'teach' her how to do the same. Every second was agony, and worse, I was feeling him teach her how to do this to me over and over again.

By the end of the lesson, he had tightened my noseband so much I felt as though I was gasping for breath. The feeling made memories of smoke and fire and scarred lungs flood back into my mind almost sending me into a blind panic. This O'Dowd saw as a positive thing, because I was rushing faster. He mentioned getting draw reins as well as spurs and I felt my life shatter. My joy at being with Hannah was being marred by this man, this professional, and her mother.

Chapter 44

I loved my hacks with Hannah. They were bright spots in my life, highs that were contrasted by the horrible lows of any lesson with Deirdre. I hated those. I hated O'Dowd with his yelling and pushing. He'd often 'hop on' to show Deirdre how she 'should be doing things'. That was even worse. He'd dig into my sides with the spurs, pull and tug on the reins making me gape against the bit. His answer to that was simple, put me in a flash noseband so I couldn't do it. The flash noseband wrapped around my nose in front of the bit and was fixed tight so that I couldn't open my mouth. In O'Dowd's mind he was right. I was naughty and I needed to be put right and taught a lesson. He didn't care if I was sore, or think for one second my behaviour might be down to the way he rode and treated me. Because he was a professional.

My outings with Hannah were full of fresh air, nature, and beauty. Her hands were always light, but eventually even her gentle touch made me flinch a little. My mouth hurt, as did my sides. I tried hard not to let it affect my rides out with Hannah, but it was hard. In a way those hacks were an exquisite torture. They stopped me going numb. That was both a blessing and a curse. If I were numb, I reasoned, perhaps I wouldn't feel it so much. I'd shut down and just survive. But I didn't, and I didn't because of Hannah.

I began to hate lessons so much that even when Hannah said we were going to do one together I was unhappy. Mrs. Murphy was not a professional, her qualifications and credentials were far fewer that O'Dowd's and she was his antithesis.

To my surprise the first thing Mrs. Murphy did was frown at me and ask why I looked so tight. Hannah wasn't sure so she inspected me. She identified my sore sides and slackened my noseband, noticing it had an attachment for a flash.

"My mum uses it," Hannah replied. "I don't like it."

"He won't either," Mrs. Murphy nodded at me. She was right.

Our lesson with Mrs. Murphy was worlds away from O'Dowd's. We worked on some pony games, fetching and carrying flags. She said with sore sides it was the kindest thing we could do. We started only in walk and Hannah barely had to urge me forwards to move into a trot. I liked the flags. I'd watched pony games before and found it was wonderful fun.

"He's a natural," Mrs. Murphy told Hannah. "And lovely forward going, I'm not sure why he has sore sides."

"Maybe he was kicked in the field or something," Hannah suggested.

"Maybe, he did seem sorer on one side." Mrs. Murphy didn't sound convinced.

Hannah would soon learn just how come my sides were sore and be left in no doubt about the source. A couple of days later I was reluctantly loaded up onto the horsebox and driven to O'Dowd's yard.

I had discovered something about the luxury stables with their immaculately swept yard and high-end facilities - it felt oppressive. I hadn't noticed it when I first visited, but every time I stepped off the horsebox I felt it now. The horses were quiet, heads hung. No one looked out over their stable doors. It was as if they were hiding, hoping not to be noticed, to be left alone. There was no joyful hitch in their steps when they walked or went out, no light or shine in their eyes. The horses in O'Dowd's care, I realised were numb. They were shut down.

O'Dowd met us in the arena as usual. The flash was tightened in place. Deirdre got on and we began. There were no flags and kind words of encouragement today. No, today was more yelling, more pulling and more digging into my sides. I wanted to close my eyes, lie down, and shut out the world. My attention faltered for a second and I stumbled, tripping a little over my own feet. O'Dowd roared and I flinched.

"He's not paying attention, give him a kick on!"

Deirdre did. Over and over, and when that wasn't enough O'Dowd himself jumped on to sort me out. His hands were heavy on the reins, pulling, tugging at my mouth making the sore spots there worse. He would boot at my sides and I could feel the spurs digging into me, the pain became less sharp, more a dull soreness that never stopped, even when he wasn't niggling at me. By the time the lesson was over I felt like I could fall to my knees and never leave the arena. I felt broken. My sides hurt, my mouth hurt, and my heart hurt. How could anyone treat someone so poorly? How could Deirdre not see how wrong this was?

No one seemed to notice my pain as I was led towards the ramp of the horsebox. If anything, they seemed happy. Deirdre was chatting to her friend telling her how much better I went for O'Dowd than I did for her. How good he was. I felt miserable. My misery only deepened when one of O'Dowd's staff rushed up with a pair of draw reins he was 'lending' Deirdre to help with me. I think part of me shattered as I watched her take them with a big smile.

"Isn't that nice," she said to her friend.

It wasn't nice, I thought. It was another way to torture me, to make me feel worse. I looked around at the horses being moved around the yard and the only bright thought I could muster was at least I didn't live there. At least I was going to leave this place.

Hannah was horrified when she saw me. O'Dowd's spurs had broken the skin on one of my sides and a little trickle of blood had stained my grey coat. She immediately inspected me all over and noticed a cut on the side of my mouth too. She tided them both with soothing warm water and put on cream.

"What happened to Storm?" she asked Deirdre.

"What do you mean?" Her mother replied.

"He has a cut on his side and one on his mouth. They weren't there before your lesson."

"Oh, well he was very stubborn today. Cillian had to do some work on him."

"WORK!" Hannah almost yelled. "Look!"

Deirdre shrugged. "He's a professional sweetie, he doesn't do these things without reason."

"Well, he's not doing them again!" Hannah huffed.

"Now look," Deirdre bristled. "I pay the bills, and I am enjoying my lessons so yes he will."

Hannah narrowed her eyes a little at her mother. "No one and I mean no one, rides until that's healed," she pointed at my side. Deirdre opened her mouth. "Unless you want me to call the vet and have him give you a bill to tell you the same thing."

Deirdre closed her mouth and shook her head.

"You're too soft with him," she said, but she didn't argue further. I wondered if she knew the vet would agree with Hannah.

Sadly, my reprieve was short. My side healed and lessons resumed with the addition of the draw reins. Shannon had been right about them; they were horrific and I hated every second in them. Hannah's outburst at the spurs did save my sides a little. I noticed after her intervention I wasn't kicked as hard with them.

Chapter 45

I was expecting to go with Hannah one Saturday morning for our usual ride, only to find myself confronted with Deirdre. My heart sank. She proceeded to clean me and braid my mane. It could mean only one thing; I was to compete – with Deirdre. Sure enough, shortly afterwards the horsebox rumbled onto the yard and I was loaded onto it. I knew we wouldn't be jumping, not with my injury, and a braided mane coupled with Deirdre's presence made a long-distance hack unlikely. I was left with two options, I was either going to a show or to do dressage.

We arrived at a pretty little equestrian facility and parked alongside a smattering of other horseboxes, too few for a show I realised. Dressage it was. Deirdre unloaded me and tacked me up, taking me to a warm up area to begin my torture. As usual I was kicked at and yanked, and as usual there was nothing to be done about it. I resigned myself to the inevitable.

I had little chance to see much of anything before our turn came. We were summoned into a ring with a car parked at one end complete with judge. Deirdre began her usual tugging and booting as she asked me to contort and perform and tuck my chin into my chest. I tried my best, but everything ached and I felt as if I could hardly breathe. I wondered if the judge would notice my discomfort. For a second, I thought this might improve my life. Perhaps the judge would tell Deirdre she rode awfully and it would make her think. I shouldn't have got my hopes up.

Once the test was over, I was dumped with a hay net by the horsebox while Deirdre and her friend went to get food and drinks and watch the other horses. I sighed as I watched too. There was a steady stream of horses paraded into the ring, many looking as sore and stiff as I did.

"Look at that." I glanced over to see a large almost black gelding with a thick white stripe watching a pretty chestnut step into the ring. "Stiff as a board and I bet she'll score well."

"Can't they see it?" I asked.

The gelding whickered a mirthless chortle.

"I've been doing dressage for twelve years now, and I tell you, half the judges don't see a darn thing.

Take my human," he glanced inside the horsebox where a middle-aged woman was sorting out the horsebox so it was ready for her horse.

"She's the kindest, gentlest rider. Lovely hands, always asks the right way for collection. Proper collection mind you. Do we win?" he shook his head. "Nope, usually a third, maybe fourth. And why? Well because someone comes along with a poor horse bent into submission with draw reins or such."

"I hate draw reins," I admitted.

"All horses do," he replied.

"I once overheard some man talking about them, a fellow doing dressage. He actually said he knew the things hurt his horse but he still used them because it makes the horse look good quickly and he scored higher in his tests. He forced his horse to tuck its head in, rather than collect properly, and he was rewarded for it."

"It hurts my neck," I admitted. "My human, well, my human's mother actually, her trainer told her to use them."

"Ah, one of those," the gelding huffed. "They're the worst. The trainers who say to use these things with no thought of us."

"I hate them," I sighed.

"Yes, and it's a habit hard to break. Why, when I first came to Roz I was constantly bunched up and tight, it took her years of work to help me learn I could stretch out again."

"You're lucky," I glanced at his human.

"I am," he replied.

Deirdre was seemingly pleased with her result. We came 6th, which she decided wasn't too bad for our first time out together. She enthusiastically showed O'Dowd at our next torture session with him. He glanced at the sheet and only picked up on one thing.

"Needs more collection," he read. "Better get some more draw rein work in. That'll help."

My heart sank. The judge hadn't noticed my predicament, if anything her comments had made it worse. I felt lower than I had since I stood starving and alone in the field.

I was, however, about to have my spirits lifted a little. It was the summer and Hannah wanted to do Saddle Camp. For a week I would be away with her, with no lessons with O'Dowd and no riding with Deirdre. In fact, Hannah insisted her mother not ride or have a lesson for the week before the camp or the week after. Three weeks of heaven.

Camp was wonderful, even if I was stabled and not turned out. I was surrounded by children and teens, all equally excited and all with their ponies. The air buzzed with anticipation. Mrs. Murphy was our teacher for the week doing two lessons a day ridden, and two lessons in horse care around muck outs and meals. As usual Mrs. M as she liked to be called, was spot on in everything she said. She held little competitions doing points of the horse, using me as her canvas. I liked that, though it tickled when she pointed to my girth line.

On the afternoons there was often jumping, but knowing I was injured, I either did tiny jumps with Hannah, or simply went around the fences with her practicing jump position. Every care was taken to make sure we were happy and healthy.

One morning Mrs. M had a workshop on collection. I listened interested on her idea of what it was and how to get it.

"Now, collection is not having your horse tuck his nose into his chest. If he does that, he can't breathe properly and he is using all the wrong muscles. It's actually hurting his body.

What we want is him to transfer a little weight from his front legs, to his hind legs. The way we're going to do that is by practising some exercises like shoulder out and shoulder in. When we get our ponies to step one hind foot under their body more deeply, it changes their balance and posture for the better!

When we get this little weight change, the angle of your pony's hindquarter will change. And then naturally their back will round a little more, and you'll see your pony naturally lift their withers and round their back. That's the proper way to start collection and help your pony's body feel strong, powerful and athletic!" she clapped a hand on my bottom and the children giggled.

"If his nose feels like a lead weight he isn't collected and he isn't balanced. And we don't want rein rein rein. You should never pull on the reins, and your horse should be taught not to pull on you! We don't want to block that forward movement, we allow it. Collection doesn't mean slow. We want flowing free rhythm and lots of energy! Now, I have exercises to do this that we'll practise. This isn't an overnight goal, this is a thoughtful 'practise makes perfect' kind of thing. Remember, your pony's nose should be either vertical or slightly ahead. It should not be tucked into his chest. Never EVER pull on the reins to try to get your pony to tuck in his nose. That's not collection, that's just bad riding."

"What about," I heard Hannah almost whisper. "What about draw reins? My mum uses them. Are they ever good?"

"Never," she glanced at me. "Quick fixes, shortcuts and gadgets that force horses to do things are never good for the horse," she stressed. "May I ask why she uses them?"

"Her instructor told her too, Cillian O'Dowd."

One of the girls a few ponies down laughed. We all looked at her.

"Sorry," she snickered. "It's just, I had a lesson off him once on Z. Z ditched him in five minutes flat."

I glanced at the roan pony she sat on. Zorro, or Z as he was called, was barely 14.2hh, he was a mix of breeds with enough Arab to have a slight dish and a high set tail. We all knew he was a little flighty, but the idea of a pony chucking Cillian O'Dowd left me awestruck.

"What happened?" Hannah asked.

"I told him he shouldn't get on. Z doesn't like other people riding him," the girl fussed the roan's neck and he snuggled into her hand. "He didn't listen."

"He never does," I muttered.

"No, he's an arrogant little toe rag," Z glanced at me. "I was more than happy to introduce him to the ground where he belonged."

"You really threw him?"

He nodded. "It wasn't even hard to do."

"How did Z throw him?" One boy asked.

"He got on," Z's human said. "And he tried to trot around the school. He wears spurs and he kicked Z." she looked angry.

"Anyway, Z didn't like that. He rushed at the corner of the school, and, well he ran at the corner, stopped dead, dropped his inside shoulder and jumped sideways. O'Dowd went straight out the side door and landed in the dirt. I laughed. I caught Z and told him that's not how he should be ridden. You know he tried to tell my parents Z was dangerous. My mum laughed in his face and said Z took good care of me every day, and that he should learn how to ride a pony!"

I thought Z's human's mum sounded brilliant. It crossed my mind that I should try ditching O'Dowd in the dirt, but I doubted Deirdre would react like Z's humans had.

Chapter 46

My lessons with both O'Dowd and Mrs. Murphy continued, and at least Hannah noticed the difference in my attitude to both. When Deirdre rode, or had a lesson on me, I would move awkwardly, pin my ears back and bunch. It even got to the point that I'd scowl at her when she came near me, associating her with draw reins, whips and spurs.

By contrast when I was ridden and fussed over by Hannah, I would constantly have my ears forward, or swivelling about so I could listen to her. Radar ears Mrs. M called them. Deirdre commented that I didn't like her as much as Hannah. Hannah chuckled at that, but there was a lot of truth in it. I didn't like Deirdre at all.

Although I was still sore when I worked with Hannah, I tried hard not to show it and to enjoy and appreciate our rides. Hacking might not have been so pleasant with a stiff neck, bruised sides, and a cracked mouth, but it was still hacking. It was still freedom and nature and a soft hand.

One morning, shortly after a rather unpleasant encounter with O'Dowd, I overheard Deirdre talking with one of the new ladies who had come to the yard. She was an event rider. I'd seen her and her mare in the school before jumping and doing dressage. No hint of draw reins used, and she was careful jumping too. One of the good humans, I decided. The lady was called Orla and her mare Flite. They were preparing to do some big competitions and as part of that Orla was organising a dressage clinic. Hearing that Deirdre was interested in dressage she asked if she would like to join in.

Deirdre seemed a little nervous when the woman talked about the clinic, and I came to realise it was because Orla had hired not just a professional, but one of the leading dressage riders in Ireland, to conduct it. I perked my ears up wondering what a leading dressage rider might think of O'Dowd's methods, but then found myself worrying they might agree with him and have Deirdre double down on her riding style.

Orla did convince Deirdre to do the clinic though, and so, one Saturday morning, I found myself saddled, bridled, draw reins in place, ready to show one of the best dressage riders around what I could do. I flattened my ears as Deirdre got on and tossed my head. We entered the school with Deirdre sat proudly in place on my back. The lady instructor took one look at us and frowned.

"We'll have the draw reins off for a start please," she stated. I perked my ears up.

"Oh, I need them," Deirdre whined. "My trainer, Cillian O'Dowd, he told me to use them, otherwise he won't collect."

The instructor took a deep breath.

"Well, he won't collect with them either, but he'll probably give you a hefty physio bill eventually. Let's just get these out of the way," the instructor began to strip my draw reins off to my utter joy and Deirdre's astonishment.

"Right, that's a bit better, let's see him go."

I stretched out and walked around the ring while the lady instructor gave out orders. She didn't yell like O'Dowd did, and all her orders were directed at Deirdre, not at what I was doing wrong. It felt much more like a lesson from Mrs. M and I found myself quite enjoying it. My ears didn't flatten, my pace picked up and I found I could move. It seemed to surprise Deirdre.

"Much better movement," the instructor encouraged. "There, did you feel that, that was proper collection."

A slightly out of puff Deirdre nodded. "Yes."

"Hard work, but proper collection, and the more you do it, the more you practise, the easier it gets."

She pulled me into the centre for a moment so she could talk to Deirdre. She fussed at me as she did. "Much better."

"Much harder," Deirdre moaned.

"Yes, but that's your fitness. The more you both work correctly the fitter you both get, and he'll not end up sore. Just because he can't speak to you and tell you verbally he doesn't like something, doesn't mean he isn't trying to tell you in another way. Look at the ears, the movement. He came in rigid ears pinned back. Now he'd working with his ears forward and his movement is much more flowing. As riders, as owners we have an obligation to do the best we can for our horses. To treat them well, care for them, ride in a kind way, and sometimes, hard as it is, make tough decisions on their behalf. We must do this because they can't speak for themselves. We speak for them."

Deirdre nodded again. "Maybe we can wean off them. I mean, I don't want other riders laughing at me just throwing them away."

"Why would they laugh? What business is it of theirs? If anything, you should be laughing at the folk using them because they can't get a horse to collect properly. Don't be afraid of other riders, set a good example, do things right. Hopefully they'll learn from it."

The rest of the clinic went well. I actually didn't mind riding with Deirdre for the first time, although given the redness of her face at the end, I'm not so sure she felt the same way.

We still did lessons with O'Dowd after that, but there were no draw reins. Hearing that someone as top notch as the clinic lady say Deirdre shouldn't use them was enough to dull O'Dowd's enthusiasm for their use, at least with me. He tried to say that the draw reins must have worked and we didn't need them anymore, and that was why the clinic lady had told Deirdre to remove them. But I'm not certain even Deirdre believed that story.

A few weeks later though, as I prepared for yet another session with him, something odd happened. Instead of Deirdre turning up with her horsebox as usual, one of the stable girls came to turn me out. At first, I assumed Deirdre was busy with something and had rescheduled our lesson, right up until Kath, one of the girls working called across the yard.

"Is he going out? Doesn't he normally have a lesson today?"

"Yeah," Erin called back fastening my head collar. "But she was getting lessons off that Cillian O'Dowd, wasn't she."

Kath bustled over. "Is that the horrible man from the internet?" she asked rubbing my neck.

Erin nodded. "Yep, caught on camera beating a horse until it flipped right over. He's up in court for it. I reckon they'll ban him from keeping horses and no one in their right mind will take a lesson off him after that."

"I wouldn't have anyway," Kath muttered. "Did you see the spur mark he had?" She nodded in my direction. Erin shook her head. "Right on his side, bled and everything. No way I'd take a horse to someone who said that was ok." She looked at me with a smile. "Fine, pop him out."

Erin led me out of the stable towards the field. "Bet you're glad there's no lesson, eh?" she patted me. I was. I really, really was.

Chapter 47

For a little while my life was alright. Hannah became my primary rider, Deirdre only appearing every now and then on warm days when she fancied a little jaunt. I loved riding with Hannah, doing horse riding club days, hacks, and small shows when she felt like it. Life was good, right up until Hannah was preparing for college. Emma had been insistent that she would only go to a college where I could be close to her, but Hannah didn't seem to have the same concerns. She was determined to go to the best school she could. My proximity was secondary.

In the end Hannah was accepted on a great course, for her. She gleefully left for college and left me behind. For a little while Deirdre showed up and exercised me, but as the weather turned cooler, she began to come less and less. I knew what was coming. At least, unlike with Aoife I was cared for. The staff at the yard fed me, rugged me, dried me and turned me out. They even brushed me a little. I wasn't in a sorry state so thin I looked starved, but I was once again human-less.

One morning a horsebox arrived and I was loaded onto it and driven away. I knew I'd been sold again. Neither Deirdre nor Hannah came to say goodbye. For all those rides and hacks, for all the care she gave me, at that moment, as I stepped onto the ramp, I wondered if Hannah had ever really loved me. Memories of Emma sobbing as I was taken away stood out in my mind in stark contrast to Hannah's absence.

The horsebox didn't take me to another yard but to the auction. At the age of 19, I was once again at the sales. I found myself surrounded by horses, some young and scared, some my age, ridden and hopeful, some older and quietly resolved to fate. Mingling among us were a huge number of potential new owners, looking around and sizing us up. I wondered where my life would take me this time. I hoped, I prayed, it was somewhere nice.

I watched many horses sold that day. Some I knew just by looking at the humans who took them, had fallen on their hooves. Others I pitied with all my heart. I realised I had learned to love and fear humans in equal measure.

My turn came and I was taken into a ring and paraded around. There weren't so many people bidding on me as had the first time around. The winner was a teenage boy who seemed extremely pleased he had won. He had a kind face and a mop of blond hair with a few bits of hay in it that I sucked out as soon as I had a chance. He laughed at me and gently pushed my nose away, giving it an affectionate rub.

"This your one then, Flynn?" A stout older woman with a jolly face asked him.

"Yep," he grinned.

"Right, well, I have one more to bid on and then we'll get going. Why don't you go load him up on the horsebox."

Flynn took me to a large horsebox and loaded me on board. There were three other horses and ponies on it, and a little later, a fourth arrived. None of us knew what was going on, or where we were going, but the jolly lady seemed nice enough so we hoped for the best.

I was unloaded at a little yard in Wexford later that evening. There were with two large schools and several horses were being ridden in both of them. I quickly realised I was at a riding school. There were children everywhere. I was quite excited as a group rushed around to meet me.

"Is this your one Flynn?"

"Did you buy him?"

"Are you keeping him here?"

"I wish I had a pony of my own."

"What's his name?"

Flynn laughed and held his hands up at the gaggle of kids. "Yes, this one's mine, yes I did buy him. Aine said I could keep him here for free in exchange for mucking out and wrangling you lot," he laughed. "And his name is Storm."

I was escorted by Flynn, and the children who all wanted to pat and fuss me, over to a large shed with a lot of stables in it. He put me in one with a rubber floor and a dusting of shavings as well as a hay net.

"You all watch him for me for a minute while I go get him fresh water and some food."

"Ok Flynn," the children chorused.

They huddled around my door each one wanting to touch my nose and fuss me. I tried to make sure they all got a chance soaking up the attention. I had a feeling I was going to like it here.

Eventually the children all left and Flynn chuckled as he brushed me clean and put a thin rug on me. "Peace at last, eh?" I rubbed my head on him and he laughed.

The other horses began to troop in, and as I watched them, I caught sight of a familiar figure. My eyes widened and I let out a shout to my old friend Seamus. He turned to see me and called back.

It wasn't until the next morning that I had a chance to talk with him. We were brought out and tied up under a little porch to be brushed and rugged before being turned out. He told me he had been at the school for a few years now, and he loved it. The school was, as I had thought, a lovely happy place full of laugher and children. Seamus was owned by the jolly lady called Aine who owned the place. He often led hacks out with her and was very content. He told me I should be glad Flynn bought me too. He was a nice young lad, Seamus said, who was training to teach at the riding school when he was older. He didn't have much money, but Aine was helping him out. That's how he had been able to afford me. He worked for my keep. Like Emma, I thought. They had a lot in common. That made me hopeful.

I asked about the others, Hamish and Shannon. He was quiet for a moment. Hamish, as far as he knew was still with Chloe, but Shannon was gone. He heard she had an accident at a yard in Meath, there was nothing to be done to save her. I felt my heart break a little. Shannon had been almost as important to me as my mother and Nana had. Knowing she was gone made my world a little darker. I couldn't help but think about my other friends. Were they still out there somewhere? Were they happy? I realised I always pictured them alive and well in my mind. I couldn't do that anymore with Shannon.

Chapter 48

Life at the riding school was good. I quickly made friends with a lot of the ponies. We mostly lived out, unless there was very bad weather, or there was an injury. There was not a spur, tight flash noseband or draw rein in sight. In fact, I learnt quickly that they were banned in the school. The instructors were kind with both children and ponies.

The school had rules about lessons. A pony could do no more than four lessons a day, one advanced, one novice, or as I saw them, one hard, one slow, morning and afternoon. There was at least an hour break at lunch and everyone was out in a paddock if they weren't scheduled to be worked in either of the sessions. All horses had at least one field day per week with no work and Monday was paperwork day so everyone was free. I was not used in lessons, unless Flynn was in the class, or there was an emergency. I covered for a lame horse sometimes. The advanced classes were alright, the riders were kind with soft hands, but I secretly preferred the novice ones when the tiny kids would sit on me and be led about by Flynn. Often, they'd try to kick me on when we did a trot, but their little feet didn't hurt and either the instructor or Flynn would remind them to nudge not kick, and to make sure they looked where they were going, which pleased me.

Flynn was a good human, and a nice owner. He treated me with care and compassion, rode with light hands and a laidback manner. I felt good again, and I felt loved. Flynn evidently cared for me, he was forever sneaking over to fuss me, pass me a carrot, or just give my nose a rub. The children loved me too. I often had a swarm of them around me, especially when I was in the field by the little shed they used for snacks and drinks. When I was there, I'd hang out by the fence for hours just having them talk to me and fuss over me. I heard countless times how they longed for a pony like me. These tiny humans, I thought, could one day grow up to give ponies homes. Good homes.

Hanging around by the school let me listen in to the lessons too. I liked that, I could hear what Aine was telling the children and I liked what I heard. She would talk about how ponies and horses were never bold. They could be cheeky, and they were very clever, but never naughty. If they misbehaved it was due to being sick, sore, confused, or possibly taught the wrong way in the first place.

"Don't get me wrong, some ponies are a bit wayward. Doughnut..." she pointed at a rotund little palomino pony. "I'm looking at you." There were giggles. "We all know Mr. Doughnut will cart you into the feed room and stuff his head in a bin of pony nuts if he gets a chance." More giggles.

"That being said, what can we use to motivate Doughnut?"

"Food!" The kids shouted and laughed.

"That's right, food. We can use food to help us train our horses. What else can we use?"

"Em, scratches?" a little girl called.

"Scratches, yes, ponies like scratches. Any other ideas? What else do the ponies like as a reward?"

"Loves and hugs?" a little boy called.

"Loves and hugs are good," Aine replied. "How about listening to them? That would be good, wouldn't it? If we listen, we can help keep our ponies happy. Ok, I want us to all think of one way we can listen to our ponies, shout it out and then trot to the back of the ride."

A procession of children called out ways they could listen to their ponies better. Everything from how we moved, our ears, how we looked, if our tails were swishing. It went on as every child took a turn to trot around the arena. Aine was simultaneously teaching them how to ride and how to listen. I was in awe.

Flynn, it turned out, had been taught by Aine from being as small as some of the kids in the class I had watched. From six years old he had been taught how to care for horses as well as ride, and it showed. I was brushed, fed, cleaned, ridden carefully, it was as if I had entered another world. We hacked, sometimes with a lesson, sometimes alone. Either was great.

When we were alone, some of that feeling of freedom seeped back into my life. Rushing wind through my mane as we cantered a bank, the spray of water as we jogged through a stream. Likewise, I enjoyed the long, easy-going hacks escorting a lesson. I often brought up the rear with Seamus at the front and a little line of pony mounted children in between.

I'd been at the school a little while when Flynn attempted to jump me over a cross pole. I tried to do it, but it was just a little too large and my old injury hurt, just a little. Flynn noticed immediately and called Aine over. She checked me over.

"He had an injury listed, yes?"

"Stifle, but it said he did jump over that height."

Aine nodded. "Might have but they didn't notice he was in pain after like you did. Well listened," she smiled at him. "Let's keep it to polework for now and when the vet comes out for the flu and tet rounds we'll have him take a look. Might be that's too high, might be we need more stretches and physio. Jenny is coming out for that in a few weeks anyway."

Flynn smiled and gave me a hug then took me over and untacked me. "Best give you a bit of time before we do anything else and make sure you don't get sore." He rubbed my nose.

I was amazed. Flynn had felt a slight stiffness in one leg. Deirdre hadn't noticed when I was so stiff, I could barely move. I took a moment to check myself over. Nothing hurt. For the first time in a long time, other than my stiff stifle, I felt good. I didn't have a sore mouth or a stiff neck from side reins. My sides weren't bruised. As Flynn led me to the field and popped me out to rest, I thought I might have actually died and gone to heaven. This. This I decided I hoped, I prayed, I dreamed, would be my forever home. I could live with Flynn. I started to imagine him doing his tests and teaching for Aine. In my mind I saw me living at the school until I was old and stiff, surrounded by the throngs of little happy children that loved ponies and wanted nothing more than to love and fuss us.

I knew, of course, that the riding school ponies didn't retire there. Seamus had already told me that once they reached a certain age, they were sold on by Aine, usually to riders who had learnt at the school and were looking for their first pony, or who had developed a special bond with one of the school horses. I though, I was owned by Flynn, like Seamus was owned by Aine. I knew her horses weren't sold on, because the horse who had preceded Seamus, a tall bay by the name of Dime, was still at the yard and retired to a life of pasture and grooming. I could be like that. I hoped.

Chapter 49

I was now 20 years old, and yes, life at the riding school was good. I finally had a human of my own again, one who owned me, treated me well and who I enjoyed riding with. My home was tidy, safe, and full of friends. I was happy. I started to feel safe again, settled.

All that came crashing down one day though when one of the children, a fairly new pupil, fell off and was hurt. Aine was very apologetic to the parents and took great care to make sure the boy was alright, getting him attention right away, but it didn't help. Only a few days later the letter came. The child's parents were suing the riding school.

I knew something was wrong instantly. Everyone seemed tense, except for the children, blissfully unaware of what was happening. Flynn however knew exactly what was happening, and I knew from his look and his mood it wasn't good. He began to chat to me about it when we were alone, mucking out or on a trail ride. I didn't quite understand what he said about lawyers and courts, but I began to get the idea as he rambled on. Flynn didn't seem to like that big corporations, or councils, or courts got to decide the fate of a riding school when so many people were depending on it.

"They just want money," he huffed. "They don't care about the kids that need this place. For some of them the school is the highlight of the week. Heck, little Tilly, she lives at the stables in the summer. Her parents are too busy with work and just drop her off. She spends every day here sweeping, grooming. What happens to her if this place is gone?"

I wished I could answer him. I realised, not for the first time that little humans were often in the same position as horses. They knew what was right and wrong but their lives were ruled by adult humans. Maybe that's why children and horses get along so well I thought.

Aine fought the case. Flynn told me she would, but he often looked concerned and mentioned money. On top of the amount she was having to pay to hire lawyers, there were other problems too. Flynn mentioned something about extra paperwork. By his account the council, who issued her a license to be a riding school, had decided they needed to know more about the place. We began to be weight taped regularly, which I didn't understand. If I lost enough weight in a week to show up on the tape, I was pretty sure someone would notice and call a vet. Aine's business rates, whatever they were, went up too, and there was something about limiting what the children could do on the yard as well.

"It makes no sense," Aine moaned to Flynn one morning. "Those kids are safer here than out on the streets doing lord knows what." She looked angry.

In the end, after months of going to and from the court, Aine won her case, but the school was on a shoestring. The money it took to fight her cause, and the time it took to go through the courts took its toll. The extra paperwork, the sky high bills and restricting health and safety regulations bit hard too.

One morning she gathered all the staff with tears in her eyes, and I watched from the paddock as she cried while she told them the school would be forced to close. Her money was gone, and even with the case won the bad press had affected the school's reputation, it was over. I think my heart broke and I knew all the children felt the same when the news spread.

Many of the kids were distraught, worried about what would happen to their favourite ponies. I worried about them. Where would they go? Would they find a new riding school? Was there another close by? Or would they be all hanging out on the streets that Flynn suggested weren't good.

I looked over at their sad little innocent faces, the gift of riding was being snatched from their tiny fingers, and with it the chance for them to grow up to be kind, gentle, understanding horse owners. Closing the school not only affected them, it affected us too. We were losing potential good human owners.

I was worried about me too. My life with Flynn was based on me being kept for free in exchange for working for Aine. With the school closed he couldn't keep me. I knew he didn't have the resources. In the end Aine found homes for several of the school ponies with kids she had taught, but there was no one to save me. Flynn tried hard not to cry when he loaded me with the other ponies not rehomed onto the horsebox. I caught a brief glimpse of Seamus as I reached the top of the ramp. The one bright spot was that he at least would stay safe with Aine.

We were once again at the sales. Flynn stayed with me, unwilling to part with me, hopeful I found a good home. He talked to anyone who came my way, talking me up to those he thought would look after me, but I knew it wouldn't be his choice who chose me.

Several horses were stalled near me at the sales, one though shouted my name and I looked over to find myself staring at Oscar. I rushed to him hoping he had news of Emma. He looked older, a little plumper, but was still cheerful enough.

"Oscar," I greeted him with a wicker.

"Oh, I am pleased to see a friendly face Lir," he replied. I started for a moment. It had been years since someone had used my original name. I'd grown used to Storm, though I never quite felt it was right. "Even if it's under poor circumstances."

"What are you doing here?"

"My owner lost her job. She tried to sell me privately, but, well, she didn't have much luck. You?" he asked.

I glanced at Flynn. "The same, I guess. My boy lost his job. Did you come from the old yard?" Oscar nodded. "How is everyone? Daisy?"

"Daisy was sold too, but she's landed herself a nice place with a family, they have five children. She's doing pony lessons with some of the older ones and some of the littler ones are learning to ride on her. I'm pretty sure she has a home for life. They own the farm she lives at, and there's another pony there too, an old retired Shetland."

"Emma?" I asked.

"She went to university, just like she said she would, to do Equine studies," he looked at me with sad eyes.

"She still came to the yard, helped out and sometimes even rode me round the track if my owner was away. She wasn't the same after you left though. She was so sad all the time. I've only ever seen one other human look like that, and that was Wizzy's mum."

"Why?" I asked. "What happened to her?"

"Oh," Oscar sighed.

"Wizzy colicked one night. It was awful, he was so uncomfortable, sweating, trying to roll all the time. The vet came gave him medicine, but it didn't work. His mum took him to the vet hospital, did lots of tests, but, well there was a problem, something that couldn't be fixed unless they did surgery. A growth I think she said. Even with the surgery the vet wasn't confident it would cure him. She asked several vets, they all told her they would do the same thing in her position. In the end she, well..."

I nodded my understanding. Another of my friends had gone.

"It broke her, doing it," Oscar went on. "I watched her sob into his old horse rug and cradle his headcollar. She said over and over how awful and guilty she felt, but you know, if I ever find myself in that state, in that kind of pain, I hope someone will put my needs first, do what needs to be done even if it hurts them."

He shook his head. "I hope someone one day loves me so much they are sad and miss me that way. The way Emma and Wizzy's mum were." He glanced around the sales at the horses lined up waiting their turn to be paraded.

"I'd love to be loved and missed so much."

I couldn't disagree with him. The thought of Emma being so upset hurt my heart, but part of me was glad to have been loved so much by her that she was affected by my leaving. I thought about Wizzy's mum too, how much she loved him and took care of him, bringing him his Christmas stocking that morning at the farm. I knew she would be lost without him and could only imagine how hard it would have been for her to let him go. I thought too of Siobhan when she suggested putting Murphy down for no other reason than to be able to afford a newer, younger horse. She would have felt no guilt putting down someone healthy, while Wizzy's mum felt awful just ending his suffering. Humans, they were complex and diverse, I'd known that already, but I was still seeing examples of it.

I was still reeling from my news of Emma and Wizzy when my turn came. At 21 years of age, I was paraded around the ring, used to it by now. People bid on me, but not so many. The winner was a short portly man with a flat cap. He seemed to be disinterested in paying me any attention when he came to the little stall to collect me. Flynn hugged me goodbye and wished me the best of luck. I turned back to him as I was led away. My hopes of a home for the rest of my life with the boy were broken. I was 21 now, age creeping in and my hopes for a pleasant forever home more forward in my mind. Glancing at the man in the flat cap I doubted I'd found it.

Outside I was loaded onto a large horsebox with several other horses ready to be ferried to our new home. I saw Oscar through the window as the horsebox loaded up. He was being put onto a trailer by an elderly looking couple and a little boy of around eight. The boy looked so excited, one hand grasping the lead rope. Good luck my friend, I wished him as we pulled away and I lost sight of him.

Chapter 50

Since I was bought with several other horses, I tried to convince myself I was going to another riding school, somewhere like Aine's. In my mind I saw myself as one of the school ponies helping the children to learn how to ride and treat horses well. In the end though I found myself at a trekking centre in west Mayo.

At first, I liked the idea of the trekking centre. It was a place where all you did was hack. That sounded alright. No stressful competitions, just nice rides through the countryside. I imagined myself doing rides like I had with Flynn and Seamus, trailing along with happy cheerful children. My daydream faltered though when I spotted another horse from my past coming back from a ride.

Star had been a cheerful pony the last time I had seen him, passed from family to family, but always to someone else looking for a pony of his talent. Now though he looked worn out and tired, as he plodded onto the yard, a man clearly too tall for him perched uncomfortably on his back. I hardly recognised him.

"Get them unloaded and stabled," Flat cap barked at a young girl.

I was lucky enough to find myself stabled next to Star when I was finally unloaded and instantly began to ask him about my new home, hoping he would tell me it was fine, but he'd had a bad day. I suspected though that in truth something bad had happened in Star's life. He turned to me, his sad, tired eyes not even seeming to recognise me.

"It's me, Lir!" I said.

He brightened a little. "So it is."

"How did you get here?" I asked.

He hung his head. "I was outgrown, so my human sold me to a riding school."

"Really? I was in a riding school. I loved it."

He looked at me stunned. "I hated it. Going round and round hour after hour. Whipped when I didn't go fast enough," he shuddered. "The place was closed eventually and they sold me here, called me bombproof."

"But, here is ok, right?" I asked.

He muttered something and then turned away to nibble at a small hay net. It didn't fill me with confidence, but I tried to shove my concerns aside. I wasn't Star. I'd liked Aine's. Maybe it would be ok here too.

My first day though I knew this wasn't Aine's. I was shoehorned into a saddle that pinched my withers and a bridle that pulled my bit a little too high in my mouth. It was uncomfortable, and that was before the weight of a rider was added. The trekking centre was nothing like Aine's, I realised. My hopes were dashed.

At the end of the first trek I stood sore and dispondent once more in my stall. Star spotted me looking forlorn.

"Why do our saddles not fit?" I asked.

"It's not his fault," Star sighed. "The old man who owns us. He doesn't know about saddle fitting, and even if he did I doubt he has the money to have it done. He tries his best I suppose but he doesn't have the money for much. Almost no one comes by in the winter. He has to earn enough to keep us for the whole year, in the decent weather, there's not much beyond that."

I gradually settled into my new life, though I can't say I enjoyed it. We would do several long treks a day with a little break between them. On hot days we'd go down the steep trails to the beach. I'd often feel my legs wobble as we struggled onto the sand. I'd barely have time to cool down from one ride before the next would begin. I could feel my mind numbing to the world. My bones and muscles ached. The nature I loved to hack around in became nothing to me, because I spent little time enjoying the scenery. I was too tired to do more than trudge along and try to keep my footing. Sometimes I wondered if my eyes had gone as dull and lifeless as Star's had.

The tourists that came didn't seem to notice any of this. I wondered how they didn't notice our tired looks. Did no one come by and look at us with concern, with pity? Could they not tell that we were becoming little more than objects, our life, our spirit, our personalities draining away?

The staff however did care, they would try their best for us, but with the limited funds available it was never quite enough to make us comfortable. They had each rider sign a waiver to protect the centre and then pushed them onto one of us. Often, they put people on me that were too heavy, I knew they could tell this, but there was nothing that could be done about it, we all needed the money. I'd feel my legs buckle under the weight of large men, or heavy-set women. Being a little taller it was rare I got a child. I tried my best to keep going, to keep these strange people safe, but each day I felt myself slowing down, my legs ached as I walked, and began to hurt even when I simply stood still.

We were fed, but not much, sometimes we got some chaff, but mostly it was just slices of hay. There was never quite enough. I was hungry and I felt exhausted, as if my body didn't have the fuel it needed just to keep me going, let alone while carrying a heavy load. I knew it was because we couldn't afford more, but it didn't help. Sometimes the staff would bring in apples and carrots for us. I learnt quickly those of us who were affectionate got a little extra and made an effort to flick my ears forward at them and behave when they handled me.

In the summer we were virtually never out in the paddocks, not unless the weather was grim and no riders were around, or we were lame. Often, we'd pray for heavy rain, although we would be soaked through with no chance of a rug to stave off the damp, we at least found ourselves free for a little while. Grass helped keep me going, perking up my energy levels a little though our paddocks were small and overgrazed. My life became the trails we trudged or the stable I used. I struggled to get moving in the mornings, to make my legs work.

As the summer and damp autumn weather turned into the biting cold of winter once again, I began to find life even more hard. My first winter at the trekking centre had been bad enough, now though I felt the aches from the summer turning into actual pain. The occasional trip down to the beach became torture as my legs hurt so much. I must have started to look really bad because eventually one of the staff suggested I be looked at by the vet.

I knew I was skinny. My bones ached, and I knew that there was little chance of there being money around to help me. The vet who came out examined me with little enthusiasm and then turned to the man in the flat cap who had purchased me from the sales. It was one of the only times I'd seen him since I'd been bought. The vet shook his head.

"He's got arthritis. What he needs is more turnout, less work and some medication."

The man with the flat cap looked me over with a sad expression, he shook his head. "Sounds expensive."

"Well, if you want him to be sound and move," the vet said with a shrug. "It's what he needs."

"I can't afford medications for him," he looked at me sadly. "I wish I could. I wish I had money for more feed, and everything, but I don't have it. The coffers will be bare by spring as is, and no one is going to come trekking in this weather."

He paused. "Could I loan him over the winter, bring him back in full work in the summer when it's warm?"

The vet sighed and looked at me. "Honestly?" he shook his head. "The cold will exacerbate the arthritis, but even in the summer he'd be sore and stiff without intervention."

Flat cap sighed and shook his head. "I can't afford it."

I felt my heart skip a beat. Was this it? Was he going to do what Siobhan would do? Was I to be put down, not worth anything to a human anymore? Flat cap called a girl over.

"Stick him in the paddock, see if you can find a rug for him, something that can keep him warm a bit and find out when the sales are on next," he stated. I started to breathe again. Sold on. It was better than the alternative. Wasn't it?

Chapter 51

So, once again I found myself at the sales. When I looked around myself, I saw many older horses, sad, tired, broken. I wondered if there had been so many the past times I had visited and I hadn't noticed, maybe we only notice the other horses like us when we arrive there I mused. Now I was 22 I saw more older horses, just as when I was 4 I'd seen a lot of youngsters.

I pondered our existence. What had brought us all to this point? What of the humans who had dumped us here in our old age? Had they abandoned us after years of work simply because we were no longer useful to them? I supposed they had. I wondered where we would end up. Would someone with kind hands come and take us to green pastures, or were we bound for death?

I knew the likelihood was most of us would end up somewhere unpleasant. We would be sold for very little. Set to end our days unloved. My mind wandered to Wizzy, his broken owner sobbing over him after staying with him to the end. Oscar was right. There were worse ways to go. What would become of me? I began to feel small and alone and afraid.

Humans mingled amongst us, most drawn to the horses that were young and fit. Few looked our way, and those that did worried me. I absently wondered if this was my end. If my last decent human contact would have been with Flynn at the riding school. I tried to cling onto the better parts of my life, hoping the memories would chase away my fears, but what should have been comforting only made my situation worse. Those who would have loved me for my all of life had been torn away by fate. Those who could have cared for me chose not to.

I heard the faint sound of someone saying my name and my ears flicked for a second. A dream. My memories playing tricks I thought, because, for one second, just for a moment, I had thought I heard Emma. My head dropped again, sure that it was my mind playing a nasty joke.

No, there again, I heard Emma's voice. I would know it anywhere. Somewhere in the crowd I could hear Emma. Would she know me, would she remember? I was useless to her, I knew I was, but if Emma was here... If I could just see her one more time, feel her hands, even for just a moment then I would be set free. I may end up who knows where, but I would have seen my Emma again first.

I lifted my head up and looked around a little frantically. I called out. "I'm here! I'm here. Emma!" My whinnies were high and loud as I bellowed with everything I had, praying she would know it was me. I looked all around and through the crowd of people I saw someone stop. A woman turned towards me.

Taller, older, but unmistakably Emma.

Her hand went to her mouth and suddenly she was pushing through the crowds of people, rushing my way. She darted to me, tears streaming from her eyes as she scrambled over the little pen gate that fenced me in and threw her arms around my neck, burying her face in my neck.

"Lir, oh Lir, I thought I'd lost you forever," she cried.

She stepped back wiping tears from her face, she smiled and ruffled my forehead. A man followed by two small children appeared by the gateway. Emma turned to him, still wiping tears from her pink cheeks.

"Cormac," she smiled at the man. "It's Lir, my Lir."

"He doesn't look much like his picture," one of the little girls pipped up.

"He will," Emma smiled at me. "When we get him home and fed and tidied up."

Home? Did she mean it? Was she really going to take me home with her? My heart leapt. She brought me forward and I stiffly followed her.

"This is Cormac, he's my husband, and this is Cara and Kate." She introduced me. Kate, the smaller girl reached her hand out and I stuck my nose on it before licking her fingers. She giggled.

"I guess we're not looking for a Shetland pony companion then?" Cormac chuckled.

Emma shook her head.

"I'm sure Lir will let the kids sit on and walk around the paddock, he's better than any Shetland."

I nudged her gently. "Besides, I have a client who offered to let me teach the kids on her grandkid's pony in exchange for a free lesson."

I pricked my ears up. So, she had done it, she'd become an instructor, one who cared about us. About me. I nestled into her, soaking up the joy of being back together.

"Sounds good to me," Cormac smiled. "Welcome to the family Lir. Oh, well, if we win."

I suddenly felt worried again. That was right, I was at the sales, people bid on horses, and while I was no longer worth what I had been, it was possible that Emma could lose me. My heart sank and I began to worry all over again. Emma wiped the remaining tears from her checks and smiled at me.

"I'll be right back."

She climbed out of my pen and marched off leaving me with Cormac and the girls. Both children sat down by my pen and I began to play with them, nudging them gently and rubbing my bristly nose on their heads. It made Kate giggle. I loved the sound, like music to my ears.

A few moments later and Emma returned with flat cap. She smiled at me and pulled an envelope out of Cormac's pocket, taking out several bills and handing them to flat cap.

"That's more than fair," he nodded. "Here's the paperwork."

He handed over a little book I'd seen the vet stamp when he visited.

"Pleasure doing business with you." Emma didn't look like it was a pleasure at all, but she said nothing and flat cap walked away, out of my life forever.

Emma opened the gate and stepped inside, she slipped a headcollar on me and gave me another hug. "This time," she grinned.

"This time you are mine and nothing, nothing is going to change that. I promise you're home for good."

I stepped slowly and a little stiffly out of the pen, but with Emma there I felt the aches less. I walked away from the sales knowing I had a home for life. I was safe, I was with Emma. I had my human back and I was happy beyond words.

Chapter 52

That was how I found myself back where I started, looking out over the field towards the Galway coast, the sea and the sand. It still surprises me how fate brought me back here. I'd seen Emma last in Kilkenny, but like me, she had fallen in love with Galway and its coastline.

She would often tell her children the story while they groomed me. Emma had come down on holiday one year and felt unexpectedly at home. It helped, I suppose, that her husband came from Galway too.

Emma still takes me to the beach now and then, when the days are warm and I'm not so stiff. She leads me, and Cara and Kate take turns in 'riding', sitting on me like little peas on a drum as we wander across the shoreline and splash a little in the waves.

Emma is teaching her children the right way to treat a horse, and I have become as much Kate and Cara's as hers. They brush me, love me and care for me. I have medicine when my arthritis is bad, long days of turnout and a lovely warm stable, with thick deep bedding when it's cold, bundled in rugs and leg wraps so my joints don't ache.

I wish my whole life could have been like this, but if nothing else I am grateful my life will end this way. One day, hopefully in many years yet, I will pass in this green pasture looking out to the sea my ancestors swam through on that stormy night, desperate to survive. I will be loved, I will be missed, I will have been cared for until my last.

I wonder some days about those other horses at the sales not so lucky as me. Then I am doubly grateful for my life and for Emma. I am not the only horse in Emma's life. Far from it. There are client's horses whose lives she tries to improve by teaching their humans the right way.

There is Bryn, the Welsh pony Kate and Cara ride on when they have proper lessons and who, if I am not mistaken, Emma is seriously considering joining our herd, though I suspect Cormac doesn't know this yet. Then of course there's Quinn, my Connemara field mate. Young and bay and full of wonder at life. He has barely seen the world, while I have seen more than I had wanted to.

"Who's that?" Quinn broke through my memories.

I turned back away from the sight of the coast in the fading light to see Emma walking towards us with two other women, one grey-haired, the other a brunette. Kate and Cara followed behind with two small boys playing tag. I whinnied and turned to walk towards them, Quinn beside me.

"That's Lucy," I replied. "And her daughter, Clare."

"Lucy who was sick?" he asked.

"Lucy who was sick," I confirmed.

Emma, I explained, had been looking for me for years. All that time while I was out there, she never stopped trying to find me. She put me on the internet trying to get news of me, and she updated everyone when she finally did and brought me home.

One of those following our story was Clare. She reached out when she discovered Emma had bought me back, now once a year she comes to visit bringing Lucy and her two sons Finn and Aiden. I had brought them together, these women who loved horses. That thought made me happy. I got a Christmas card every year from the children too, and a bag of horse sweets wrapped in bright paper from Lucy and Clare. It was proof positive I was loved. We wandered towards the gate.

"Does that mean you know what happened to your Shetland friend?" Quinn asked.

I realised he had listened to my story, not just eaten the grass as I had half expected. "You mean Dougal? Yes, I know what happened to him. He ended his days the way we all hope to. He died in his sleep at the grand old age of 32, loved by Jilly right up until he took his last breath in a warm stable after a day in a green pasture."

Quinn paused as if taking in what I had said. I heard him mutter, "That's how I'd like to go," as I marched on towards Emma, Lucy and Clare.

"There he is," Lucy laughed as I walked to her. She scratched my neck.

"Still a handsome man." She turned to Emma. "I'm so glad you found him again. The stories I bet he could tell."

"I'm glad I found him too," Emma smiled at me. "If it wasn't for Lir I'd never be the instructor I am today. I owe it all to him."

"He always was a special one," Clare fussed over me. "I said that to Mum way back. I wish I could have kept him for you when you were sick," she hugged her mum.

"Then he wouldn't have met Emma and we'd have one less good instructor in the world," Lucy pointed out patting Clare's arm. "More horses will have happy lives because of that."

I pricked my ears up hoping Lucy was right. The sun dipped a little further on the horizon, casting shadows across the field and making the blades of grass pink tipped. The sound of the children playing and laughing filled the air, the scent of the ocean drifted to my nostrils on the gentle summer breeze. Yes, I was loved. I was happy.

I had found my home.

Glossary

An Garda Síochána – the name of the Irish police force. Also knows as the Guards.

Bars of the mouth - the two sides of the lower jaw where the bit lies.

Broken (broke) - When a horse can wear a saddle and bridle and carry a rider, a horse can be called 'broken'. When a horse is ridden, you can also say it has been 'backed', or 'started'.

Cavesson - A cavesson is a tool for groundwork, and consists of a type of headcollar, without a bit, but with 3 rings that are attached to the noseband (the band that goes around the horse's nose).

Cavesson noseband - A cavesson noseband is a simple band that goes around the horse's nose. It is kind to the horse.

Draw reins - Draw reins employ a pulley mechanism to prevent the horse from holding its head too high, by lowering the head when it moves beyond the desired position and maintaining it in that lower stance. There are 2 reins, one on each side. They start in the rider's hands, run through the side of the bit and then are attached to the girth under the horse's stomach. When the rider pulls on these reins the horse is forced to tuck its chin towards his chest. They restrict the horse's movement.

Figure of 8 / grackle noseband - This works in a similar way to a flash noseband and looks like a figure of 8. It restricts the horse opening its mouth.

Flash noseband - A flash noseband is a cavesson type noseband, with an extra strip of leather which is tightened around the horse's mouth. It restricts the horse opening its mouth. It has become popular in the last 20 years.

Gelding – a male horse that has castrated, which is a surgical procedure performed by a vet.

Groundwork - any training you do with a horse when there is no one riding the horse. This can include walking beside the horse, long-lining, teaching the horse how to step sideways or backwards and lots more. It's a very effective way to start teaching a horse new movements, and getting a horse out in new places to build their confidence. The horse may wear a headcollar, halter, cavesson or bridle or nothing at all.

Hands – How to measure a horse or pony's height. 1 hand is 4 inches. A horse that is 15.1 hands tall is 61 inches tall.

In-hand work - this term is similar to groundwork, and is sometimes used interchangeably. It often refers to work done in a bridle with a bit and reins, but without a rider in the saddle.

Liberty work - any training you do with a horse where there is no tack on the horse and the horse can move independently by themselves.

Long-lining - often done with a young horse before they are ridden. The horse wears a bridle and 2 long lines are clipped on each side of the bit. Then the rider walks holding these lines, behind the horse, and the horse walks on ahead. Traditionally this is done for a few weeks or longer to help a young horse to build up confidence in new places and to get them used to the signals from the bit.

Side reins - Side reins are two leather reins, one each side, that attach from the bit to the saddle area. The goal is to force the horse to carry its head and neck in a certain position. They restrict the horse's movement.

Tied up – muscle cramps, which tend to affect the large muscle areas of the horse, like the back and hindquarters.

Weaned – the process when a foal is separated from their mother.

More books by the #1 award winning author, Elaine Heney

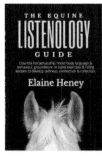

www.elaineheneybooks.com

Enjoy the exciting new

CORAL COVE
CONNEMARA PONY SERIES

by Elaine Heney

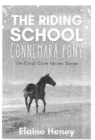

www.elaineheneybooks.com

Printed in Great Britain
by Amazon

45226258R00199